Box of
Letters

ROB CARMACK

93 Days of

Devotions for

Teens

•

WINEPRESS **WP** PUBLISHING

Packaged by WinePress Publishing, PO Box 428, Enumclaw, WA 98022. The views expressed or implied in this work do not necessarily reflect those of WinePress Publishing. Ultimate design, content, and editorial accuracy of this work are the responsibilities of the author.

Unless otherwise noted all scriptures are taken from the Holy Bible, New International Version, Copyright © 1973, 1978, 1984 by the International Bible Society. Used by permission of Zondervan Publishing House. The "NIV" and "New International Version" trademarks are registered in the United States Patent and Trademark Office by International Bible Society.

ISBN 1-57921-307-3
Library of Congress Catalog Card Number: 00-103123

Introduction

When I was seventeen years old, I spent the summer in Fort Worth, Texas. Throughout that summer, I became close to a young seminary student named Greg. It was through Greg that God called me into full-time Christian ministry. Through Greg, I received many opportunities to use my gifts to serve God and help people along with their own spiritual lives. I am thankful God has used me to minister through music, speaking, and now writing. I look forward to seeing the plans God has for me in the future.

It has taken me over a year to complete this work of devotionals. The first of these was written because there was a brief time in my life when I had lost my passion for leading music. It was in this time that I began looking for another way to serve God and minister to people. One late, sleepless night I began to unload my thoughts on paper. Bursting with ideas, I desperately needed a way to vent them. So, I booted up the old computer and went to work. It was these writings which led me to begin working on a daily devotional book.

In my "quiet times", I have gone through books similar to this one. I found some of them very helpful and insightful, while others left me with a bad taste in my mouth. I have always wanted a daily devotional book that would take the way I felt and put it into words with a biblical solution.

I began to think if I didn't write it, nobody else would, though I don't think of myself as a writer. I am much more effective communicating person-to-person. However, I am confident God has given me the opportunity to help people in their quiet time, and I am thankful for this.

This book is entitled *Box of Letters,* because I see each page as a message from my own life, which can hopefully be applied to yours. Even though I may not know you, I am writing these "letters" for you, so you might be able to use them to draw closer to God. I pray they succeed.

I cannot take full credit for what you will read in these 93 devotionals. God has inspired me and gracefully used an unworthy servant to deliver these messages. In doing this, He has placed people in my life, without whom I would have never persevered to finish what seemed at times to be an unending project.

Instead of writing out a long list of names, trying to thank everyone who has contributed to this book, let me simply say thank you to everybody at once. If I have ever spent more than five minutes with you, you have contributed. To the people in my hometown of Hinton, Oklahoma, thank you for raising me. To the people of Bear Valley Community Church in Colleyville, Texas, thank you for teaching and using me. To the people of Prince Avenue Baptist Church in Athens, Georgia, thank you for accepting me, even when you didn't know me. And to Greg, thank you for taking the time to be my friend and mentor. I owe so much to all of you and cannot thank you enough for inspiring my life as you have.

And thank you, reader, for picking up this book. I hope you grow and learn as much through reading it as I did through writing it. God bless you.

Quiet Time

*"After he had dismissed them, he went up on
a mountainside by himself to pray. When evening came,
he was there alone,"* Matthew 14:23

One night, I was on the phone with a friend whom I had not talked with in quite a while. When the topic came to church and things of that nature, I asked her when she had last had a quiet time. I was distressed and a bit disturbed when I received the response, "Didn't we do that at church camp?" How is it that this bright, intelligent, young lady had never really known what it was to spend time with God? So, for those of you who are in the same boat as my friend, let me lend you a hand.

What is a quiet time? It is not like the "time-out" your parents might have used to discipline you as a child. This is a time for you to be by yourself; try growing and learning in your relationship with the Father. Some people get up early in the morning to do this, while others wait until before they go to sleep at night.

"But what do I do?" Personal quiet times vary from one person to another. You could read the Bible, pray, or read through a daily devotional. Many people like to write in a journal during their quiet time, because it gives them a chance to reflect in words and on paper. However you chose to do your quiet time is fine, as long as you're authentically striving to know God better and walk closer with Him. Making time for God is a vital part of any growing Christian's daily walk. It should not be like doing homework or mowing the yard. You should savor and look forward to these times.

These quiet times are the foundation for a growing relationship with Jesus Christ. They give believers a chance to truly experience the grace of God in their lives.

Have you been spending enough time with God? Do you sometimes look at your quiet time as a chore? How have your quiet times been going?

Speechless

"How great is the love the Father has lavished on us, that we should be called children of God! And that is what we are! The reason the world does not know us is that it did not know him." 1 John 3:1

L et me ask you a question: Have you ever tried to verbally describe a sunset to someone? Or have you ever tried to tell someone how beautiful and breathtaking the ocean is? Every time I go to the beach and look out at the endless horizon, I am completely blown away. It is something I cannot even comprehend, much less describe to someone else.

One summer, I was teaching a small group at a camp, and I was trying to find a creative way to describe God's infinite love, mercy, grace, and power at one of the sessions. Let me tell you that it was tough. I could not find a suitable analogy even close to describing all of the incredible attributes of God.

Then, it hit me. The more I read and studied and prayed, the more I realized all of these wondrous things could not be described in words. My heart began to beat fast in my chest, and my mind was going faster than I could process (this often happens when I have a revelation of this magnitude). We cannot describe God's power and love because it goes way beyond what we could ever understand.

Think about it for a second. Why would anyone give up a perfect life in heaven to live on earth and die on a cross? How is it that the God of the entire universe rejoices over every lost soul who is found? Quite frankly, I just don't get it! It leaves me in complete awe. I am humbled and silenced when I sit and truly consider all that God has done for me and how wondrous his grace really is.

So, I finally realized that before I can be fully equipped to teach others about the grace and love of God, I have to allow myself to be overtaken in awe of all God is and does. Before I can teach, I have to be taught. Before I can speak, I have to allow myself to be left speechless.

Have you ever come across a time when you were completely floored by all that God is and does? If so, what was it like for you? Have you ever taken a step back to allow God to leave you speechless in his infinite and perfect grace? It is a humbling experience!

The Love I Know

*"This is how God showed his love among us:
He sent his one and only Son into the world
that we might live through him." 1 John 4:9*

Like the couch potato I am, I was watching one of my favorite weekly sitcoms with a main character in a therapy session, stressing about one of his current predicaments. At the height of his ranting and raving he shouted, "I *knew* God would never let me be successful!"

"I thought you didn't believe in God." His therapist said.

He looked at the doctor and simply said, "I do for the bad things."

I know this scene was meant to be funny, and, honestly, I did get a laugh out of it when I first watched the episode. But the more I thought about it, the more I realized how much this television character represents a lot of people in the world—including many Christians.

Why do so many of us get angry with God when things go bad? I don't know about you, but I have done this myself. I can remember thinking, "God, how could you . . .?" or "God, *why* would you . . .?" Most of us are guilty of blaming God for our problems.

Some people are even convinced God is out to get them, much like the character on the TV show. They are so paranoid that God is rubbing His hands together and toying with them for a good laugh. This, obviously, is a big mis-conception. This notion is just the opposite of the truth.

The truth is we are loved beyond our mere comprehension. If you don't really believe that, look at the price he paid to forgive us of our every sin. And if the traditional Easter story doesn't fully help you appreciate the love we are given, ask a historian or a pastor to describe to you what the crucifixion process really involved. An accurate description of what Jesus went through could actually make your stomach turn.

We need to realize God wants the best for our lives and does not desire to harm us in any way. His love is a powerful thing and is not to be taken lightly. It is a love that only those who know Christ can truly experience.

Have you ever felt angry with God? Why did you feel that way? Have you ever felt God wasn't looking out for your best interests? Do you really understand He always wants the best for you? Are you thankful for the love God offers you?

The Change

*"Therefore, if anyone is in Christ, he is a new creation;
the old has gone, the new has come!" 2 Corinthians 5:17*

Have you ever felt some people view Christianity as a fashion statement? Just think about it for a second. We have our Christian T-shirts, cross necklaces and key chains, all sorts of catchy bumper stickers (e.g. "Honk if you love Jesus"), and our "WWJD" bracelets.

Don't get me wrong. There is nothing wrong with any of these items. But please understand there is more to being a Christian than wearing a cross around your neck. It's about being a follower of Christ.

You see, when someone receives salvation, they are "a new creation." There is a change in them which nothing else could bring about. I once heard a speaker say that the evidence of salvation is a changed life. How true that is! I have been to discussion group after discussion group, and I have always heard people give inauthentic answers to spiritual questions. They would have the right answer, but the meaning was lost. Now, having all the right answers to the world's toughest questions can really help you in school, but in spiritual examination, it's just a bunch of hot air.

I was one of those kids who always had the right answers. I grew up in church and had gone to Sunday school my entire life. So, the tough questions were always easier for me. But there was no change. I was a T-shirt Christian. That is, until a warm September evening in 1997, at a revival in my home church in Hinton, Oklahoma. I answered the altar call and prayed with my pastor. I realized what I lacked was not spiritual knowledge or more T-shirts, but the true grace and love of Jesus Christ. Since that evening, I have been a new creation.

Once again, don't misunderstand me. All problems and struggles did not vaporize as soon as I said, "Amen." I still struggled, and I still had to deal with things. I still had temptations to face, but it was easier now. There was someone there to pull me up when I fell. People noticed a difference in me, as well. I was, in fact, a new creation. I finally had the change.

Have you ever felt you were living your life as a "T-shirt Christian"? Do you ever feel you are lacking the change, which God's grace offers? Do you know anyone who needs this change? If so, pray for them today.

I Don't Want To Know

*"No one knows about that day or hour,
not even the angels in heaven, nor the Son,
but only the Father." Matthew 24:36*

We live in an age where everyone wants to know the outcome of the future. We, as people, are so impatient about the future that we have to know everything right now. Look at the people who put their faith in psychics, palm readers and their horoscopes in the daily newspaper. For some reason, we need all the answers now.

This is a little embarrassing, and I really don't want to share it, but it's so relevant I feel I have no choice. When I was sixteen, I had been having a discussion with one of my teachers about prophecies on the millennium and the end of the world and all of the other junk attached to this topic. Soon after that discussion, I had a dream. This dream led me to believe I knew the exact date on which I was going to die . . . June 1st, 1998. I was very superstitious (and not very bright) at the time, so I believed it was true. This tormented me for *months*. I thought this was a true vision until the clock struck 12:01 A.M. on the morning of June 2nd. I decided then that I would not be superstitious any longer, and I would allow God to control my life instead of false prophets and astrologers.

Why are we so pressed to figure it all out? We think we have to know when the end will be and how it will occur, so somehow we can save ourselves. If you are searching for an answer and want to know the exact days of the end times, I hate to be the one to burst the bubble, but we *can't* know. Read the verse at the top of the previous page. No one knows the day or hour. The Bible also says He will come "like a thief in the night."

It's time we realized that God's timing is perfect, and our impatience will only make things more nerve-racking and crazy for ourselves. We should be patient and learn to wait for God. Don't be so wrapped up in how things will end, but spend more time thinking about your life, day by day.

Have you ever wondered how this will all end? Have you ever let it bother you and keep you up at night? What conclusion did you come to? Have you ever tried to be patient and let God do things in his own time?

If You Want to Lead Me to Jesus

*"And what does the Lord require of you? To act justly
and to love mercy and to walk humbly with your God."*
Micah 6:8

L et's pretend you are not a Christian. It's not that you
lead a particularly *bad* life; you have just never been
too interested in the whole "church thing." One day, a
person you are acquainted with, but don't really know too
well, invites you to go with them to their Wednesday night
youth service at church. You aren't really interested, but
you've got nothing better to do, so you go. You really like
it. The music is good, the youth pastor seems like a nice
person, and the message on salvation gets you thinking
about things. Could it be that Jesus is what you've been
looking for all along? You are honestly interested in pursu-
ing this idea. You are so interested and anxious you cannot
wait until you get the opportunity to have all of your questions answered. The next day, you spot your friend and walk
toward the group when all of a sudden, you catch a small
bit of their conversation. Possibly, a guy is talking crudely
about a girl he was with last Friday. Maybe a girl is gossip-
ing about another person who didn't come to school dressed
as fashionably as she did. Whatever they are talking about,
it definitely does not correspond to what was being said

last night at church, and it rips you in half. You retreat, dismissing all thoughts of someday becoming a believer in Jesus. You thought Christians were supposed to be different. And the truth is, we are.

Now, I have a question with a simple but distressing answer: Why is it when people are confronted about Jesus or Christianity, their natural reaction is to roll their eyes, scoff, and even laugh? Now, here's the horrible answer: *It's our fault.* We, as Christians, sometimes treat our relationships with God like a part-time job. We know all the answers taught in Sunday school, and we can talk about it until we're blue in the face. But more often than not, we are potentially embarrassing to God by living our everyday lives with the attitude that we shouldn't even care who is watching or how they are affected. We must live our lives as examples for Christ. Sometimes we are the only real representation of Christ those around us will see. My challenge to you is: Lead people to Jesus in what you do every day, not just how you act on Sunday and Wednesday.

Do you feel like you sometimes do things to make people think twice about Christianity? How does it make you feel? Do you care?

The Race

"Do you not know that in a race all the runners run, but only one gets the prize? Run in such a way as to get the prize." 1 Corinthians 9:24

When I was a freshman, I was a member of my high school's cross-country team. The 5-k race was, physically, one of the most difficult things I have ever attempted. Practices were grueling, and the actual meets were even worse! There were times when the pain of having to run such a distance seemed almost too difficult for me to bear. But no matter how much pain I was in or how much I wanted to give up, I still ran and would always strive to win.

It is the same for us in our daily lives as Christians. We have a race to run, and, as difficult as it sometimes seems, we must always strive to win. We train by spending time with God daily, reading His word, and learning to apply it to our everyday lives. We run when we are living life. If you are striving to win the race, you should be trying to show people that the word "Christian" isn't only a tag for people who attend church on Sunday mornings.

One part of cross-country that I remember the most is the utter discomfort I went through every time I set foot on a course. I would find myself running with a side-cramp that felt as though a dull blade had penetrated the skin of my stomach. My legs would ache and throb. The winter air was so cold it made my sweaty hair freeze to my forehead. And to make it all worse, my school-issued cross-country shorts were shorter than any person should ever have to wear. Needless to say, I was uncomfortable! But, oddly enough, I still ran.

We should do the same and get out of our comfort zones. It is necessary if we want to successfully run this race of the Christian life. This could entail things such as inviting people to church, picking up someone's books if they drop them in the hallway between classes, offering a smile to a stranger in the hall, and anything else you can do to show the love of Christ to someone else. The simple fact is this: Everyone needs Jesus. It is our job, as Christians and runners for Him, to lead people in the right direction. And by doing this, we are running this race to win!

How do you feel you have been running your race? Do you sometimes feel you should be running when, in reality, you are walking?

The Thread

*"Though one may be overpowered,
two can defend themselves. A cord of three strands
is not quickly broken." Ecclesiastes 4:12*

Have you ever taken a good look at a homemade quilt? It's really interesting and amazing that such a wide, spread-out object could be made up of so many smaller, less valuable pieces of cloth. If you notice, most of the squares on your average hand-made quilt don't look anything like the other cloth squares. Now, stay with me for a minute or two. Keep visualizing that quilt, but think of it as a body of believers, or the church. Each square represents an individual Christian. You might notice there is one thing which holds all of those square pieces of cloth together, a piece of thread.

Do you see where I'm going with this? There are many different types of squares, or Christians, in the body of Christ. You have musicians, public speakers, teachers, firemen, athletes, doctors, police officers, writers, and the list goes on and on until the sun comes up. Despite how different we are from each other, and how little we have in common in the workplace or school, we should all be held together by the same thread, which is Jesus Christ. Sure, there will be differences of opinions and very rarely will everyone agree on everything, but if we have allowed God to be the bond who truly holds us together, everything else will be solved according to His Will. We should strive to build a strong relationship with those who are in our churches and our communities, to grow and love each other as we were intended to do.

Yes, we need a firm relationship with God, which is very essential. But what is almost equally important is that we have the fellowship of other believers. They are there to lift us up, encourage us, and hold us accountable when we mess up. They are the other pieces of the quilt which are held by the same thread we are. That thread is God. Remember, without the thread, the quilt would be worthless. It would just be a lot of small, individual cloth squares. The same goes for us. Without God, the body of believers is worthless. He holds us together, draws us closer, and makes us effective to do His will.

Are you close to other Christians in your community? Do you feel you help each other in your walks with Christ? Do you feel fellowship with other believers strengthens your relationship with God?

Next Five Minutes

*"This is the day that the Lord has made;
let us rejoice and be glad in it."* Psalm 118:24

L et me share with you a couple of bad habits I have carried with me through the years. The first is I spend too much time remembering events and things which have already happened. I spend so much time reveling in the past, I forget to savor moments right here, right now. The second habit that needs work is that I spend too much time concentrating on future events. For example, "What will I do next summer?" or "What classes will I take in the fall?" Things like this also take away from my enjoyment of the here and now. If I spend too much time on the "already" and the "not yet," I will not get to experience this very day God has made and given me to use. We can never have these moments back once they are gone. God has given you this day as a gift.

I once became so wrapped up in a past event and wanted so badly to recreate it as best I could that I let days, and eventually weeks, slip right through my fingers. This has happened more often than I would like to admit.

Don't think I am saying it is wrong to reminisce or plan ahead. On the contrary, I think both are very important.

One of the greatest learning tools you will ever have is the memory of your past experiences. Also, it is very important to plan ahead for your future and consider all possible routes you may want your life to take. The message I am trying to get across is we should not spend so much time on these things that they control our lives.

Every moment God has given us is precious. We are not guaranteed another minute, much less another day. Remember, the next five minutes may be your last five minutes on earth. So, make the best of them, and make every minute count!

Have you ever felt you spend so much time worrying about the past or future that you lose track of here and now? If this were your last five minutes, what would you do with them?

I'm Third!

*"Jesus replied: "'Love the Lord your God
with all your heart and with all your soul
and with all your mind." This is the first
and greatest commandment. And the second is like it:
"Love your neighbor as yourself.""" Matthew 22:37–39*

L et's face it—we live in a completely self-absorbed world. This, I'm afraid, is because we, as individual human beings, are self-absorbed people. Everyone is always trying to be first and best at everything. Now, I'm aware I cannot solve all of the world's problems, but I am confident I can at least solve mine. It's actually not as complex as you might imagine. It requires me to make a list of who comes first in my everyday life. This list should look something like: God first, the other person second, and I'M THIRD.

God first. This is to be accomplished by following all of His commandments and seeking to do all things for the Glory of God.

The other person second. Other people matter. They matter to God, and they should matter to me, too. I should be able to take the focus off of me and consider someone else. I need to ask myself, "How can I help make this person's life better?" I'm not talking about strangers here. I'm talking about friends and acquaintances. Being a better friend is one of the main keys to saying, "I'm third."

God first, the other person second, and I'M THIRD. This is a happy way to live, the best way to live, and the only way to really live in God's light. It gives us our ability to set ourselves aside and look to see if we are pleasing God, how we are affecting others, and how this will shape our own lives.

Do you ever find it difficult to adopt the "I'm third" mentality? Do you know any people who live their lives in such a way as to display this very thing? When do you best display this? How can you tell?

Hold It Up to the Light

*"If any of you lacks wisdom, he should ask God,
who gives generously to all without finding fault,
and it will be given to him." James 1:5*

R ecently, I was faced with a huge decision. I had been praying for an opportunity to minister to people over the summer and for months received no answer. But suddenly, within the span of three days, I was offered an internship at two separate churches. Now, if there had only been one job offer, the decision would have been easy, but God gave me a challenge. I earnestly sought God's will on this decision. I was so afraid to choose because doing so would eliminate the other choice, and I would be stuck. I felt I had to make the right decision. Eventually I did decide, and as I sit here now, looking back on that summer, I am, without a doubt, certain I made the right decision. God blessed my choice, because I genuinely sought His will and consulted Him on the decision. I am now staring at an even larger choice: What college will I attend? I have yet to receive an answer on that one, but I am patiently waiting for God's perfect timing.

That part is crucial. I learned to trust that God's timing is always right on schedule. I also learned if God always gave me the answer as soon as I asked the question, I would never have the opportunity to use my faith. It is an experience like this which gives a person the chance to exercise his or her faith in God's will and timing.

So, seek God's will on every decision that comes your way. Be faithful in prayer and patience, because He would never leave you hanging in the wind.

Have you ever faced a decision in which you consulted God? How did it turn out? Do you ever grow impatient and feel as though your prayers won't be answered?

Fingerprints of God

"I praise you because I am fearfully and wonderfully made; your works are wonderful, I know that full well."
Psalm 139:14

When I was in the eighth grade I was on the junior high basketball team. I practiced hard, was dedicated and had a passion to play. The only problem was the simple fact I was simply not a very good basketball player. I wasn't as fast as the other guys, couldn't make a shot to save my life and couldn't handle the ball well, either. For lack of a better word, I stunk! And I hated the fact that I wasn't good at sports, wanting so much to be able to play well. It became all right, though. There were other things I had a knack for. I learned that being an athlete—while fun and exciting—wasn't for everyone. But for so long I thought there was something wrong with me, just because I wasn't good at basketball.

Often, I've looked at myself in the mirror and seen things I wished I could change. I have always seen myself as being small and scrawny and have wanted to be bigger. But, quite frankly, it just isn't happening. Finally, I have come to recognize myself as my own worst critic.

I always find myself in conversations with people (usually younger people who are still growing and changing) who say things that are negative about their own appearance. "My nose is too big." "I'm fat." "My hair isn't pretty enough." But I ask, "Why do we have to be so hard on ourselves?" Honestly, am I really less of a person because I don't look as good as Tom Cruise? Of course not! I am exactly the way God intended me to be, and so are you.

I now realize God has been molding me since before I was even born. The greatest thing is, God is not through with either you or me yet. He is still working on us every day. We are each a masterpiece, created by God's own hands. We have on us the fingerprints of God.

How do you see yourself? Do you constantly find yourself looking to change something about your appearance? Can you see the fingerprints of God on yourself?

A Breath of Fresh Air

*"Your love has given me great joy and encouragement,
because you, brother, have refreshed the hearts
of the saints." Philemon 7*

One summer, some friends and I were hired for one day of labor. Our task was to lay sod. What is laying sod, you ask? It's when you take big pallets of unplanted grass and lay it on top of a surface that needs grass. Does it sound easy? It might, but it isn't. We spent *all day* working and laying out rolls of sod in the roasting summer heat. We worked eight long hours. When I arrived home after this long day of hard labor, I jumped into the shower as if it were my first in years. Afterwards, I picked up the clothes that I had been wearing and took a good whiff. Holy cow, what a smell! Have you ever smelled someone who has spent the whole day working out in the sun? It's a major *stink*! But, have you ever been around someone who has just taken a refreshing shower after that big stink? It's a considerable improvement. It's refreshing to smell and feel that good.

Our lives have a similar effect on people. The way we act will have an effect on other people's reactions to us. Have you ever met someone who stunk up the room with their actions and words? A bad attitude, rudeness, lack of tact, and disregard to other people's feelings can be ways that someone can stink up a room. It's not fun being with people like that. It's pollution.

But, have you ever met someone who was refreshing and enjoyable to be around? I have. My friend Greg comes to mind. He is one of those people whom every time I come in contact with him, I feel that I have been blessed by his warm and humorous presence. My pastor, Steve, is the same way. He is always so joyful I cannot help but be in a good mood in his presence. Another person who comes to mind is the famous Christian musician Steven Curtis Chapman. I had the honor of meeting him briefly one day, and immediately his kind spirit and humble presence made me instantly wish I could sit with him and absorb some of his personality. These examples are what we should strive to be like every day—the type of person who reflects Christ and refreshes the hearts of people. So, what I'm trying to say is, don't stink up the room. Be a positive example and a breath of fresh air.

Have you ever known someone who was a blessing to be with? If so, what made them so special? How do you sense yourself "smelling" to other people?

Best Days

"Then I realized that it is good and proper for a man to eat and drink, and to find satisfaction in his toilsome labor under the sun during the few days of life God has given him—for this is his lot." Ecclesiastes 5:18

T he summer I attended a church camp on the beach in Florida, I went in a van with fourteen other people from Fort Worth, Texas, and the drive took us an entire day. I want to tell you about the day *after* the long drive. All fifteen of us went to the beach for a free afternoon of fun (camp didn't start until the following day). We all spent the day swimming, throwing around the Frisbee, chatting with local fishermen, and enjoying the company of each other. I remember taking a moment to pause and appreciate where I was and whom I was with. This day was what I would call one of my "best days."

On my eighteenth birthday, my Dad and I drove from our little town of Hinton to Oklahoma City and spent the day together. We went out to eat, caught a movie, and drove around the city, just the two of us. I took another moment to appreciate that day. It was another one of my "best days."

I look back on my life and realize with little surprise at how many "best days" I've been given. We all have had those days at some point in our lives. You know what I'm talking about. These are the days when it seems like we've been dealt an exceptionally good hand at the card table of life. I love and cherish those days.

You may say that one of your best days was a good bonding experience with a parent. Maybe it was a day that you spent with a close friend. Someday, you may say that it was the day you first met your husband or wife. We should all be able to say one of our best days was when we first came to know Christ as our Savior.

One thing I have learned is to savor the good days in my life. Those really good moments need to be captured and appreciated. God gives us good, and sometimes even *great* days and moments, so let's appreciate the life He has given us. Many times in prayer I take a moment to thank God specifically for one really good time in my life. These are the gifts I am most thankful for.

What are some of your best days? Have you ever taken time to thank God for these and other moments, which truly make life worth living?

Between You and Me

"Do not let the sun go down while you are still angry."
Ephesians 4:26

Have you ever had an argument with someone who is close to you? I have. Recently, I found myself in a heated discussion with my dad. We both said things that hurt each other. Eventually we parted, angry with each other because of this encounter. Later, I went to my dad and apologized. We made amends, and not a word has been spoken about it since.

I have a feeling you have probably been in a similar situation. Maybe not specifically with your father, but with someone close to you. If you have, then you know these things can leave you restless and hurt.

The best way to clear your conscience, and do what Christ would have you do, is to go to the person as soon as you can and make amends. Without this, you may end up building a barrier between you and one whom you care about.

Now, more likely than not, as you grow to know more people and develop closer relationships with them, something will eventually rock the boat a little bit, or for that matter, a lot. You must be prepared and have already decided that when the day comes, when your relationship with someone is tested, you will be willing to lay down your pride and humble yourself for the sake of the friendship—even if the other person is too stubborn to do the same. Recompense must be made if we want to continue to have good relationships with God and the people around us.

Have you had a conflict with someone close to you recently? How did it make you feel? Have you sought to heal the relationship? Why or why not? Have you ever been asked for forgiveness? How did you respond? Was it the way you want God to respond when you need to be forgiven?

Did You Mean It?

*"So, because you are lukewarm, neither hot nor cold,
I will spit you out of my mouth." Revelation 3:16*

L et's say you go to summer camp with your church. At this camp you meet a new person of the opposite sex. The two of you spend the whole week around each other, and at the end of camp you get really sad and mushy and tell each other, "I love you and will always love you." You promise to call, write letters, and email on a regular basis. A couple of days later, after getting home and stepping back into the real world, the commitment you made to your CR (Camp Romance) is a fading memory. Throughout the following year, you maybe write the other person a letter, just as a formality, while you are sort of dating a few different people. A year passes, and you go back to that same camp to be reunited with your "true love." You tell each other that you're sorry that you messed up and didn't keep in touch as promised, but this year, things will be different, by golly! This year you're going to write letters every day and love each other forever. After camp, the past year repeats itself. Too many people today treat God like an overdone CR. I've attended various church camps over the years, and I know as well as anybody how people can get that "last night of camp emotion," where they say their relationship with God will grow. They cry and swear that their life is going to change. They testify in front of everyone from their home church that they will become active and make a difference for Jesus. But only one or two days after camp ends, it is already evident that the "deep and meaningful" commitment made to God and their peers was not worth the market value of a cheaply woven "WWJD" bracelet.

I went to a Geoff Moore & the Distance concert one night. At the end of the show, Geoff Moore led an invitation, and said with conviction, "If you're coming down to the front because you feel guilty, please . . . don't come. Because if you make another commitment and break it, it will only add to your guilt, and no one needs more guilt." Too many people are making hollow commitments to Christ and not keeping them. So, before you get up in front of God and promise to make significant changes in your life and the lives of the people around you, ask yourself one question and search hard for the answer: Do I really mean it?

How have you done at keeping your commitments with God?

Tell Us What We Want to Hear

"For the time will come when men will not put up with sound doctrine. Instead, to suit their own desires, they will gather around them a great number of teachers to say what their itching ears want to hear." 2 Timothy 4:3

I'm sure that you've seen the movie, the play, or are at least familiar with the story of that age-old classic *The Music Man*. For those of you who were left behind, the story revolves around the small town of River City, Iowa, and a smooth-talking con-artist who comes to town offering everyone things they've always dreamed of: fame, fortune, town recognition, etc. He hypnotizes the townspeople by telling them all what they want to hear.

In a line from a big Hollywood movie, one of the main characters says, ". . . tell anyone what they want to hear, and you can sell them anything." I know it was only to build the plot of the movie, but it really drives home a solid point, doesn't it? Aren't we all capable of being "suckers" if we're not careful?

Even as far back as Adam and Eve in the Garden of Eden, people have loved to hear what makes them feel good. Satan told Eve she could become like God, if she would taste the fruit from the forbidden tree. She did, and I don't have to finish the story for you.

We *love* to hear someone else tell us, "You're the best," or "You could be famous," or something else along those lines. As a musician (or at least sometimes I pretend to be), I truly love it when someone tells me they think I'm good at my instrument. One compliment from the right person can make my whole day go right. But the truth is, these flattering words can cause us to put our guard down. They can distort our judgment and our wisdom. It's all right to be appreciative and glad to hear them, but don't let them cloud your decisions and life.

In short, be careful. Whatever you do, don't lose sight of the truth. Remember, whatever skill you get praised for is something God gave to you first. And if someone offers you words that "tickle your ears" and sound like they could benefit you, read between the lines and try to look past all the enticing things being said to coerce you.

What makes your ears take notice? Do you often have trouble discerning the truth when someone is telling you something you want to hear? Do the love of self and pride often get in the way of your better judgment?

Walk with the Wise

"He who walks with the wise grows wise,
but a companion of fools suffers harm." Proverbs 13:20

Often in prayer, I ask God to grant me wisdom. I do this because I am aware of how incompetent I am without God's wise guidance and counsel. But no matter how many times I pray this, I have never found myself making a decision or in a conversation where I instantly was given wisdom.

Why wasn't I acquiring vast knowledge and wisdom? This question bothered me for a long time, because I have always believed God would answer any sincere prayer made to give Him glory, and I thought wisdom was certainly something all Christians needed to grow and learn to love the Father more.

I know people who have wisdom, though. My uncle Sam, who is a pastor, is one of the wisest men I have ever known. Both the pastor at my own church, Steve, and my youth minister, Dave, have wisdom. Even my good friend, Greg, displays wisdom I have always admired. How did these people come to be this way?

I finally got it. I was gaining wisdom. I realized I could acquire wisdom and knowledge through spending time with those who already have it. The four people I mentioned earlier are examples of people I surrounded myself with, who were good influences on my life. By spending time around them, they were teaching me what it was to have wisdom.

In the Bible, when God asked King Solomon what he wanted more than anything in the world, he answered that the most useful and needed thing the Lord could give him was wisdom. He knew that a good king was wise and discerning.

How do we acquire such a valued thing as wisdom? The answer is as simple as it is true. Surround yourself with growing believers. There are surely people in your life whom you would consider to be wise. Spend time with those people. Be willing to listen to and heed their advice. Seek out people who are further along in their spiritual walk than you are, and spend time with them. Hang out with them. Do whatever makes you comfortable around them and seek their friendship. Through doing this, you will be walking with the wise. And when we walk with the wise, we will grow wise as well.

Whom do you know in your life who has wisdom? Do you surround yourself with wise or foolish people?

When Nothing Is Left to Stand

*"But whatever was to my profit I now consider loss
for the sake of Christ." Philippians 3:7*

I went to a camp for a week with a church I had never been to before. While at this camp I met a girl who, in my eyes, was something special. We spent the whole week getting to know each other, sharing stories and enjoying each other's company. When the week came to an end, she went back to where she had come from, and I did the same. I knew I would never see her again. She lived in a place I was nowhere near. We came from two different worlds, and when we parted, I was wounded. I tried writing to her, but her parents wouldn't allow it. We were too far apart to keep in touch. I was completely crushed by this parting.

How could anything have left someone feeling so hollow? You know as well as I do when you care about something very deeply and it is lost, it can leave you empty inside. How can we guard ourselves from this agonizing pain?

If you don't mind, take a minute to list your top three priorities, preferably on paper. And please, no Sunday school answers. Be honest with yourself and recognize three things, which bear the most important standings in your life.

Done? Now, let me tell you if you wrote "God" in one of those spaces, you're on the wrong track. We seem to think God has a space in our lives, like sports, music, dating, and everything else. That is a wrong notion. God shouldn't be *one* of our priorities. God should be involved in *every* priority. If you consult Him on all of your decisions and all of your priorities, you are probably less likely to experience as much heartache and pain.

Don't get me wrong. If you wrote "my relationship with God," it is exactly the thing all of us need to strive to improve. To fervently seek and build a solid relationship with Christ is one of the greatest and healthiest things we can make as our top priority. This is not to say you won't experience sorrow and hard times, but this may better equip you to go through those times.

For me, seeking God was difficult, because I felt God had let me down and messed with my emotions. But from this came a lesson. I learned that when nothing is left to stand, God will always be there to carry me through emotionally difficult times.

Of what priorities do you not let God be a part? Why? Have you ever been broken and felt completely alone? What did you do?

Thank You, Goodnight

*"Give thanks to the LORD, for He is good.
His love endures forever." Psalm 136:1*

T here are some days I am so thankful to be alive. I feel
so thankful for all I have been given, and I just have to
say "thanks."

We should be much more thankful than we are naturally inclined to be. We spend way too much time in prayer *asking* for things: "Lord, give me this." "God, make this easier." And I am as guilty of this as anyone. But don't get me wrong. There is nothing wrong with supplication and seeking God's help, but we should be much more conscious of what we ask for and how much.

Before asking for more, maybe we should try to thank Him for the blessings we already have been given. If you have trouble thinking of things to be thankful for, let me help you. There are three things a Christian can always turn to:

1. What were you before you met Christ? If He has changed your life at all, you already have quite a bit to be thankful for.

2. Look forward. If you have received Christ, then you are "fit for eternity." Your soul has been claimed and protected for all of eternity. Remember, there is no suffering in heaven.

3. Look at your present blessings. If you can't find even one thing in your life to thank God for, you simply aren't looking hard enough. Maybe it is a good friend, a parent, a spiritual gift, or talent you have; no one in Christ is without blessing.

Once, at a weekend retreat session, our leader told us of someone whom he had challenged to go home, set a timer, and thank God for five minutes. He wasn't to ask for anything for himself or anyone else, only to be thankful. When asked how he did, the man replied that it had been one of the most difficult times of his life. It was so hard for him to think of five minutes worth of thanks to offer to God. How can we keep asking God to give us things when we are simply not thankful for what we have already been given?

I want to advise and challenge you to end each day in a positive way and take a few minutes to thank God for everything He has provided and blessed you with.

Are you thankful for the blessings God has given you over the years? With what has God blessed you this past week?

A Little Pride Issue

"That is why, for Christ's sake, I delight in weakness,
in insults, in hardships, in persecutions, in difficulties.
For when I am weak, then I am strong."
2 Corinthians 12:10

We can all get pretty high on ourselves at some time or another. Whether we're good at sports, music, speaking, drama, schoolwork, popularity or for whatever other reason a person could have for allowing his or her head to swell like a balloon attached to a helium tank; we can all be a little too proud of ourselves sometimes, can't we?

Sometimes things can hurt our pride, too. Things like being dumped by that ever-so-special person, being cut from the starting position of whatever varsity sport floats your boat, or failing a test when you were sure you would ace it without a problem. All of these things can really bruise an ego, especially one which has been highly inflated.

I am going to tell a story that I am a little embarrassed about, but it is a solid illustration. I had led music for a couple of small church groups when I was seventeen, and I had become convinced I was pretty good at it. A time came when I was going to visit one of the groups I had led earlier that year. As I spoke to one of the leaders from this group over the phone, I not so subtly dropped a hint that if they wanted me to play a few songs for them, I would be available.

Without hesitating, the voice on the other end of the line answered that they already had someone doing it, and they were doing a great job. I made it sound like it was fine, and it didn't make a difference if they didn't want me to do any music. But, in reality, it bruised my ego. It quickly knocked me off of my pride wagon and gave me a sizeable serving of humble pie.

I love to feel good about myself. Don't you? It's all right to want to be accepted. It's also okay to feel good about doing a good job. But there is a fine line between being proud of a good accomplishment and having a swollen head.

We should all realize that without God's divine grace, those gifts wouldn't be possible. We have been *given* things which make us feel worthwhile in our everyday lives. We should make a practice of humbling ourselves by realizing how inadequate we would all be without God's grace and mercy. Thank Him for the abilities and gifts that you have been given.

How many times have you patted yourself on the back and allowed your ego to swell? Are you thankful for the gifts you have?

Famine or Feast

*"Let us not become weary in doing good,
for at the proper time we will reap a harvest
if we do not give up." Galatians 6:9*

Have you ever had a moment or series of moments when you felt nothing but pure joy? How about when you finally got a car that you had been wanting for so long? Or maybe you found someone of the opposite sex who just rocks your boat and that person likes you a whole lot, too.

These are times when you smile and say a prayer of thanks to God. But what about when someone close to you dies? How about when a person of the opposite sex realizes he or she isn't attracted to you anymore, and there's someone new whom they are showing all of their attention to? Do we look to the sky and shake our fists at God, screaming, "It's just not fair"? Sometimes we truly do just that. What happened to the praise we were giving God when everything was good?

The simple but humbling truth is God always deserves our praise. We are to thank Him for what we do have, instead of complaining about what we don't. God has many ways of testing us and putting us in our place.

One of the most positive ways to pass those tests is to be thankful about *something* all of the time. You could thank

Him for the close friendship you have had with the person who is in your prayers and may not be doing so well and keep praying for them. If that special girl or guy dumps you for someone else, be thankful for the friends you have to share your pain with.

Let's face the facts. We get tired. We don't always know the answers. And yes, sometimes life is really rough. But God does know all of the answers. He can give us wisdom to know how to deal with tough things that come our way. Sometimes people get very angry with God. We say, "Because I have had it so rough, God obviously doesn't care about me anymore, so I don't care about Him anymore either." What a childish way to live.

I personally try to think of the story of Job every time I feel like I've got it rough. This guy had and lost everything, including his health. He had gone to rags from riches in no time and never once did he curse God. That takes integrity. We, as Christians, need to finally understand God is not a "fair-weather friend." He loves us through the good times and the bad.

Have you ever blamed God when everything didn't go your way?

Only a Fool

*"Do not deceive yourselves. If any one of you thinks
he is wise by the standards of this age, he should become
a 'fool,' so that he may become wise." 1 Corinthians 3:18*

When I was seventeen, I attended a church camp in Florida with a group from Texas. At this camp, we were divided into groups with people we didn't know from several different churches. Our group leader's name was Kim. I came to learn that Kim had earned her college diploma and was a certified elementary teacher who, in the middle of the year at the school where she was gainfully employed, discovered a calling into missions. She felt God was calling her to leave her teaching behind, to serve Him in ministry.

Kim was certain her parents would support her in this decision, having raised her in church her entire life. But their reaction was not as she had expected. Her father was baffled and perplexed at her sudden desire to change careers. He did not support her, and, as of that summer, they had not spoken in months.

You can imagine, as well as I, Kim's father obviously thought her sudden decision to give up the safety net of teaching to risk financial defeat was, to say the least, "foolish." Kim's father is not alone in his belief. We live in a very success-oriented world. Parents want their children to grow up to be doctors, lawyers, accountants, and, in Kim's case, a teacher. But ministry is not necessarily a successful financial endeavor.

By the world's standard, anyone willing to give up a steady paycheck to give the Gospel to people who need it is being a fool. In response to that accusation, I say I am proud to be considered a fool to the world, ignorant of the temporary happiness it can give. It has no match to the happiness I have already, in my limited experience, received through working in ministry.

Now, let me clear up one small misconception. Becoming a "fool" does not mean God wants us to stop learning. Becoming a fool means, very simply, if we want to become wise through God, we must reject conventional ways and standards our everyday world sets for us.

So, if you feel called to ministry, let me urge you to be compelled to be seen through the eyes of the world as a fool.

Do you feel called to do God's work? Are you afraid because of the possibility of failure? Are you afraid to be seen by the world as a fool?

Let Us Pray

*"Devote yourselves to prayer, being watchful
and thankful." Colossians 4:2*

Every once in a while, someone will approach me with a request for prayer. I used to look at this request as an imposition and even be irritated when someone would give me a prayer request. But eventually, I realized I should feel honored when asked to give this underestimated method of help to someone. When asked to pray for someone, we may often say out loud, "Sure, you bet," as a type of formality, without having any intent to pray for the requested person's needs. We also need to realize that we can pray anytime. God does not keep an appointment book and does not require us to schedule time to spend talking to Him.

I have a friend who is very quiet and does not like to speak in large groups. When she wants to have a conversation with me, she actually feels the need to quietly say, "I want to *reserve* some time with you today." I feel terrible she really feels as though she needs to reserve time to have a conversation, but I am reminded how blessed I am, because I can speak with God anytime I want. I don't have to reserve time or make an appointment, and I am thankful for that blessing.

Sometimes, while by myself, I pray out loud. Sometimes, I feel like there is no one listening, and I am talking only to myself. I know it's not true, but nevertheless, I occasionally have those insecurities. The reality is, God is always listening, and He always cares about our concerns, even when it doesn't seem like it. I know this because in the past, all of my sincere prayers have been answered. Sometimes the answer is, "Wait a while," while sometimes the answer is simply, "No."

We should also note that God delights in our prayers. Every time we display our faith by calling out to Him, I believe He smiles at the faith and obedience of His children. He takes joy in the fact we know we can't do things on our own and need Him for guidance and support. Don't be afraid to ask God for whatever help you need. The answer may not always be clear, but He is listening, and He will answer.

Do you feel comfortable asking God for help in areas where you are weak? Do you thank God for people who are praying for you?

Too Young to Serve?

"Don't let anyone look down on you because you are young, but set an example for the believers in speech, in life, in love, in faith and in purity." 1 Timothy 4:12

When I was seventeen years old, my friend Greg invited me to go to Florida with him for the purpose of leading music at a week-long youth camp, where he was to be the main speaker. He called the person in charge and asked if it would be all right for him to bring his own music leader. Permission was given, and before I knew it, I was signed up for what would possibly be the most life-changing week of my life.

But suddenly, reality showed its ugly head. "What if I don't meet these people's expectations?" "What if I'm not good enough?" I thought. However, the greatest fear I had was, "What if they don't accept me as a music leader because of my age?" I was only seventeen! Some campers would probably be older than me. I became afraid my age would cripple my ability to accomplish what God wanted me to do. On the contrary, when I arrived, I was received with open arms, and God washed away my fear. What a waste of energy it was to worry about something as insignificant as my age.

The legal system has created many laws and regulations that require people to be a certain age to participate. A person must be sixteen to drive and eighteen to vote. These are heavy responsibilities. But the heaviest responsibility that we are given is one with no age limit, and that is to serve God and seek to serve others. I have never heard a God-loving adult tell their young child they are too young to pray, and I have never heard a pastor say there is a minimum age to become a Christian. When it comes to serving the Lord, age is not an issue.

What difference should it make when you are serving God? When we are earnestly seeking to be faithful servants for Christ, no matter our age, God is pleased with our desires. I cannot overemphasize that when God is in control, age is not an issue. The basic message is this: "Don't let anyone look down on you because you are young." Paul understood people would not take Timothy as seriously as they should, simply because he was still considered to be a boy. As young Christians, we should not allow ourselves to be underestimated by skeptical onlookers.

When have you been frustrated or discouraged because of your age? Why did you feel this way?

Don't Walk Alone

"As iron sharpens iron, so one man sharpens another."
Proverbs 27:17

One summer, I had the privilege of taking a trip to the beach with a group from Fort Worth, Texas. Before we left on the trip, I knew I needed to be in a place where I was authentically searching for God, and I knew the beach presented certain "visual obstacles" which might have hindered me from keeping myself in focus. I asked a close friend of mine to ask me if I was "keeping my eyes straight" on the beach from time to time. He agreed.

When we arrived, as I had expected, there were quite a few female Florida natives who were more than a little generous to the watchful men when they were choosing their daily attire. (That's my nice way of saying there were a lot of women on the beach in skimpy clothes.) Our accountability method lasted a couple of hours, but after a little while, the beach, sun, and carefree fun that people are allowed to have at the beach faded-out the "eyes straight" method. It didn't take me long to realize, if I wanted to do this right, I would have to fly solo.

A day or so later, I was jogging on the beach with a friend named Jessie. We passed two young ladies walking in the opposite direction. "Are you keeping your eyes straight?" she asked me, after they had passed us. I hadn't even thought about it since the first day, but I had desperately needed someone to hold me accountable, and God graciously provided. For the rest of that week, Jessie acted as my accountability partner, and I was grateful on more than one occasion.

Some people believe all they need for spiritual growth are prayer and Bible study. As important as those things are, we need the fellowship of other Christians just as much. We need to spend time with other believers because they have the ability to truly encourage us in our spiritual walk.

As responsible Christians, we have to be willing to be held accountable, as well as to hold others accountable when they ask. If someone asks me to hold him or her accountable to something, I take it very seriously. This type of thing puts me in the hot seat. The way I see it, if I neglect to hold someone to what they ask, I am giving them an opening to stumble into whatever it is they wish to avoid. Being someone's accountability partner should be seen as an honor, as well as a huge responsibility.

Do you need to be held accountable for things you struggle with? What are they? Who could you ask to help you?

For the Sake of the Call

"Whoever serves me must follow me;
and where I am, my servant also will be.
My Father will honor the one who serves me." John 12:26

D ave Fuller was my youth pastor in Hinton, Oklahoma. When I was a junior in high school, Dave came to youth group with the message that he had been called to be youth pastor at a church in a different city, and he would be leaving in a matter of weeks. As he gave us this sad news, his chin quivered, and his eyes watered. He told us he really didn't want to go, but he felt if God opened a door for him, he was sure he was supposed to go through it.

Three days before movers were set to come to the house and carry the Fullers away from Hinton, Dave had this sudden, awful sense of dread. Why was he moving? Was he following God's will? Or was he afraid to *not* go? Dave felt now that he not only didn't want to go, but God was giving him permission to stay.

He called the other church and resigned before he even had a chance to start. He told us later he simply didn't feel at peace going to the new church. I never asked him, but I imagine Dave felt very much like Abraham, when he was about to sacrifice his only son, Isaac, and at the last minute

God said, "Wait. You have proven your faithfulness, and I know you fear and love Me."

I admired Dave's unquestioning willingness to go where he felt the Lord was sending him. He was able to say, "I don't want to go, because I'm content. But being obedient is far more important than being content."

So, like Dave, I try to listen closely for the voice of God. Not in a physically audible sense, but in my heart and soul; I believe when God wants me somewhere, I'll know it if I'm truly seeking him.

Hebrews 11:8 states: "By faith Abraham, when called to go to a place he would later receive as his inheritance, obeyed and went, even though he did not know where he was going." That's the type of blind faith that I want. Even when I don't have any idea where I'm going, I still want to follow the will of God.

The willingness of Jesus' disciples overwhelms me. When Jesus called them, they didn't put in a two-week notice. John and James didn't say they had to wait until their dad found someone to replace them on the fishing boat. With reckless abandon, they followed the call of Jesus without a question. They dropped their nets and followed Him.

Are you willing to follow wherever He leads you? Could you leave your comfort zone to faithfully follow the call of God?

Take My World Apart

*"Teach me your way, O LORD, and I will walk
in your truth; give me an undivided heart,
that I may fear your name." Psalms 86:11*

Can you think of a time when you were given a responsibility in your church or community? Did it maybe go to your head a little? If it did, don't worry, you're not the first. I too have come under the spell of feeling bigger than I really am.

It happens in sports, music, school, and pretty much any other realm of talent or responsibility that there is. This can be very harmful. But it can especially be intensely dangerous in the realm of ministry. Many times, when we are placed in a position of high regard or responsibility, even when our initial motive is to serve God, we can too often become proud and arrogant. These superior attitudes will most likely end up hurting the very one whom we originally set out to serve. It doesn't only apply in a declared ministry position. You don't have to be a missionary or a deacon to let pride get in your eyes. Every day, everywhere we go as Christians, we always wear the name of Christ. But sometimes, we end up embarrassing other Christians and ourselves.

There is a quote from an old movie in which one of the characters declares, "Nobody knows what they truly believe.

They have to guess at it by how they find themselves acting." That quote can be a harsh reality to those who have caught themselves showing disregard for the God to whom they have pledged their lives.

As we indulge ourselves in things of this world, we forget what our lives have cost—what *my* life has cost. My prayer (and hopefully yours, too) is for God to take the selfishness, weakness, and vanity I sometimes possess. Then, for Him to take my pain and tears and allow me to humbly serve Him again. The only way we can hope to apply every aspect of God's undying love is to become completely absorbed in Him. Without that type of devotion, we become significantly less useful to God's purpose.

I have to allow God to take my world apart, piece by piece, and make everything His to control. I will, without a doubt, mess things up again. Fortunately, Christ has already overcome any sin I could commit against Him, and He is always eager to forgive and willfully take my world apart.

What part of your life have you held back from God? Do you truly realize the price paid for your life? What can you do to make yourself more humble and willing to let God take your world apart?

Whatever You Say

"Many are the plans in a man's heart,
but it is the Lord's purpose that prevails." Proverbs 19:21

There was a time not too long ago when I thought I knew exactly how I could serve God best. I saw myself as a Praise and Worship Leader, and that's what I was going to be. I decided this was God's will for my life, not thinking to consult Him on the topic. I prayed for more opportunities to lead music, thinking that I needed to get started right away with my "ministry." I was sure God would use me in the area I wanted Him to use me. Of course, it didn't work out quite the way I had planned.

God took the time I wanted to be building a music career and instead built in me more patience to wait for His perfect timing and for His will in my life.

If we truly want to serve God, we must set our plans aside and openly agree to do whatever He commands us to do. We all tend to get a little ahead of ourselves and want to progress as fast as we can and do what we want to do. We may even have good intentions, but if it is not done according to God's will and timing for our lives, it is completely futile.

As I read through most of the Bible, I see God consistently growing patience in those who are called to do His work. Most of the time—if not all of the time—in those stories, when God works something to His will, it does not look at all like the original vision of the person who was called to serve. But it is always better God's way.

So, I can plan and strategize all I want, but God's plan far outweighs mine and will always prevail. His way is better, and my time is better spent seeking His plan.

Have you ever made plans and gotten into a rush without consulting God first? How did it work out? How can you be more open and patient with the Father?

There Is Only You

"You shall have no other gods before me."
Deuteronomy 5:7

A s people, we have the hardest time staying focused on one specific thing, don't we? Why is it easy to have our attention diverted from one thing to another so quickly? In this verse, God instructs His people that they are to have no other gods before Him. If there is to be only one thing in their lives, it is to be Him.

People have made a lifestyle of creating their own 'gods' from what is made available to them by the world. For some people, their idol could be the pursuit of money or a dating relationship. I know for me, there have been many times when my dating relationships have stepped in front of my relationship with God. I know many avid sports fans who would take an evening of Monday Night Football over a quiet time or a small group meeting anytime.

Sometimes, a person's job will become what he or she makes first in their life. I have struggled with this one as well. The pursuit of success and making it one step higher is an easy trap to fall into, without even realizing it. For me, being in a band was something which took importance over spending time with the Father. I loved the crowds and the music, and it was so easy to get carried away with being a real musician in a real band.

Keep in mind, these things are not bad. But there is something much more important in our lives, and that something is our own personal relationship with God. He wants to be the only one in our lives taking priority over everything else. We are instructed to have no other gods before Him. It's time for us to clear out the clutter and junk of our graven idols and golden calves and concentrate on what really matters in each of our lives.

Is there anything in your life that stands between you and a full relationship with Christ? If so, what is it?

Modern-Day Pharisees

*"Why do you look at the speck of sawdust
in your brother's eye and pay no attention to the plank
in your own eye?" Matthew 7:3*

What if you went to school one day and found an anonymous note in your locker? Let's say the general theme of this note was that you were not living your life "according to God's standard," and this anonymous person was kind enough to point out to you something they felt you needed to change. Now, let me ask you something. Would this note actually help you? Did it embarrass you? Did it hurt you? The person who wrote this lovely little note was—without even realizing it—being a modern-day Pharisee.

In case you're a little unclear as to what I mean by that, here it is. Pharisees were religious scholars who always had this knack for criticizing Jesus for whom He hung out with and what He did. They saw themselves as more righteous and better than everyone else. But they were really just a bunch of super-spiritual, holier-than-thou freaks.

Unfortunately, this self-righteous, judgment-passing attitude didn't end when Jesus rose from the grave. It still goes on today. We are all capable of being this way. We always see sawdust in someone else's eye before we see the giant board in our own. I have seen this occur many times when believers begin to feel God has appointed them judge over their peers. But we are not called to judge others. We are called to love others and be a light in a darkened world. The Bible was designed to be a light—not a hammer.

How do you think Jesus would respond to our self-righteousness of today? Have you ever found yourself pointing out faults in others while you still have a "plank" of your own to deal with? Are you a modern-day Pharisee?

Turning Rags to Robes

"And we know that in all things God works for the good of those who love him, who have been called according to his purpose." Romans 8:28

Y ou know, sometimes life will take a turn in a direction you don't want to go. Sometimes, things can start out looking pretty grim and hopeless. We all have those instances in our lives where we think, *there is no way any good could come out of this.* "God could never turn *this* into something positive." But this is the wrong impression.

I have a friend who was eighteen years old when her father took his own life. This girl was naturally shocked and seriously emotionally injured when this happened. I am confident God did not will this to happen, and it was not in His perfect plan. You could not help but think, "How in the world could any good come out of such a horrible tragedy?" Well, God was able to use Christians to bring her closer to Him. They rallied around her in love, support, and prayer. And, while this didn't cure all of her hurt and pain, it allowed her to experience a love from other believers, which she was not familiar with. Though this was an awful tragedy, God was able to work good out of it.

He does the same thing for us. No matter what happens in our lives, if we will trust God and seek His wisdom, He will take anything that seems hopeless and give it hope. He is consistent in this simply because of His unconditional love for us as His children. No matter how bad things look and seem to be, our Father in heaven can and will work good from it and make it something blessed in our lives. This is one of the features of God that I find completely astounding.

When have things ever looked like absolutely nothing good could ever come from them? What did you do? What did God do? How did it turn out?

The Mountain

"Peter said to Jesus, 'Rabbi, it is good for us to be here.
Let us put up three shelters—
one for you, one for Moses and one for Elijah.'" Mark 9:5

When Peter was up on the mountain with Jesus during the transfiguration, he saw how everything going on was great. He was so thrilled to be there with these men of God that he wanted to make camp there. I imagine I would feel the same way if I found myself on a mountaintop with Jesus, Moses, and Elijah! But, of course, they eventually had to come back down to the world below them.

Most of us have also been on a mountain with Jesus. Whether it was a church camp, retreat, Disciple Now, or some other time, believers came together to go deeper in knowledge and love for Christ.

I have spent a great deal of time on that mountain as well. And when the time comes to leave, I don't want to come down from my lofty peak. It is such a beautiful and peaceful place, designed for learning and praising God. Why would anyone want to leave a place like that? It's a place we could stay forever—but we can't do that. We are given these times to rest, grow, and learn in our faith. This is so when we come down from our "comfy" mountain to the world as we left it, which seems so far below, we can be a brighter light than we were when we left. These are times for us to prepare and spend time in intimate learning with God.

We can descend with hope and enthusiasm, because someday our Father in heaven will take us home to live on His mountain for eternity. What a wonderful day that will be!

No, I can't say I've ever wanted to leave the precious mountain I love so much, but I know with the right heart and attitude I will come back down as a better servant than when I ascended.

Where is your mountain? When have you ever felt like you were in a comfortable place, where God had put you for the purposes of resting, growing, and learning? How did you feel when you came down from your mountain?

The Blame Game

"The man said, 'The woman you put here with me—
she gave me some fruit from the tree, and I ate it.'
Then the Lord God said to the woman, 'What is this
you have done?' The woman said, 'the serpent
deceived me, and I ate.'" Genesis 3:12–13

Nothing is ever really our fault; is it? Somehow, someone else always manages to be responsible for our mistakes; don't they? It's been this way since the very beginning of time. Adam ate fruit; Adam blamed Eve, and Eve blamed the serpent. They were afraid of getting into trouble, so they naturally decided to blame someone else, to soften the blow on themselves. Why are we as humans so incapable of accepting responsibility for our own actions? Why couldn't Adam have said, "Yes Lord, I disobeyed Your only command. I'm sorry." That would have at least left him with a little bit of integrity.

Do you have brothers or sisters? If you do, have you ever blamed them for anything you got in trouble for? If your answer is no, call me, because I want to know your secret. I'll be honest. When we were little, everything I ever did was my little brother's fault. I don't think I ever got into trouble without trying to take someone down with me. As I grow older, I realize playing the blame game is not an acceptable way for anyone to live.

How easy would it have been for Jesus to look down from the cross and say, "I don't deserve this! It was *that guy* who ____!" or "Why am I even up here? *She's* the one who deserves this because ____!" (You can fill in the blanks for yourself.) He would have been completely justified in doing so, but Jesus didn't do that. He remained silent and took my blame and your blame for Himself. If Jesus could die because of our mistakes, why can't we live and accept the responsibility for our own actions? I think it's time to start.

When have you ever placed the blame on someone else when you really should have taken responsibility? Has anyone ever blamed you for his or her mistakes? Do you think people can learn to take blame for themselves?

Life as a Spectator

*"Never be lacking in zeal, but keep your spiritual fervor,
serving the Lord." Romans 12:11*

I grew up in a small Oklahoma town called Hinton. One thing we Hintonites pride ourselves on is our high school football team, the Comets. Almost everyone in town is an avid football supporter, and nearly every Hinton citizen comes to a game or two each season. They do this because they love to watch the game. Of course, very few of them actually play the sport. They don't support the game because they love to play, but because they love to watch and cheer.

I love to go to baseball games. I love the leisurely atmosphere the stands offer at your average baseball game. I love to sit back and watch athletes play the game. However, I'm sure the game is much different from a player's perspective. I seriously doubt it's quite as relaxed and laid back from the playing field. These sports are very much like life.

We are accustomed to going to church, sitting and living our Christian lives in a "comfy" seat at the back of the room. We only want to watch, because participation would be too challenging. In life, we are not called to be spectators, but rather, to be players. We are called to live a Christlike life and make a difference in our world, rather than sit in the bleachers (or pews) and not worry about it, because we've got lives of our own to lead, right?

Our generation is under the impression that we are here to be entertained. On the contrary, we are here to serve and to make a difference in our lives and in our community. So, don't be content with sitting in the stands. Get on the field, and start making a difference!

Have you ever felt like you were watching life go by while you were sitting on the bleachers? What did you want to do about it? What kind of difference are you making in the lives of those around you?

Be Still

"Be still and know that I am God;
I will be exalted among the nations,
I will be exalted in the earth." Psalm 46:10

I have a tendency to get myself all worked up about life and everything in it. Once I get going, it's like a snowball of planning and stress. It's very hard for me to relax when something needs to be done. What am I doing wrong? I need to be still.

I am also quite a talker. Seriously, I could tell story after story without even thinking about it if someone didn't stop me. I have difficulty making myself be silent.

Be still. Be silent. Stand in awe. Know that He is God.

I am really working on letting myself be still. To be able to actually stop, stand back and say, "God did that. Wow." Or, "God, the creator of this entire universe, loves *me*. Wow." And in reflection of that, be still and silent. It is an amazing thing when you stop and stand in awe of all that God is and does. The very thought of being able to truly be still, silent, and acknowledge with my heart that He is God and that He is my Father makes me tingle.

It's not easy to do. I have to shut out the whole world, lock the doors, turn off the radio, and maybe even turn off the lights. And then, I must just sit and be still, not thinking about my homework or some girl on whom I've got my eye. I must spend some time—maybe only a minute or two—being still and seeing God with my heart. We should all allow ourselves to be still to know and acknowledge He is God, with our hearts and our minds.

Be still. Be silent. Know He is God, and stand amazed in His awesome wonder.

Do you ever have a hard time stopping and relaxing? How hard would it be for you to spend a minute in silence and awe of God's wonder and grace? Have you ever tried?

Lights

*"Whenever Jesus spoke again to the people, he said,
'I am the light of the world. Whoever follows me will
never walk in darkness, but will have the light of life.'"*
John 8:12

I'm a born performer. Ever since I was a little child, I dreamed of somehow getting into the spotlight. I love to get center-stage and strut my stuff for everyone to see. I have had my share of opportunities to be in the spotlight, and I've loved it almost every time.

But sometimes, my own personal spotlight gets in my eyes to blind me and distort my perspective. Other times, my "pride light" fades out. This happens when I am shown, from a usually unpleasant circumstance, I'm not as great as I thought I was.

In the Bible, Jesus says *He* is the light. He doesn't say, "Rob is the light of the world." Instead, he says, "*I* am the light of the world." I have learned because of this, our own meager attempts at making celebrities out of ourselves is futile. This is because, as the Audio Adrenaline song so eloquently puts it, "I'm never gonna be as big as Jesus."

I saw a Newsboys concert in Dallas. At the end of the show, Peter Furler stood on the stage with thousands of people hanging on his every word and said, "Don't remember us as a band, but remember us as servants. Because we are here to serve the King of kings and Lord of lords, whose shoes I am not fit to carry." It's been a while, and I may have missed a syllable here or there, but the message is the same. We may be in lights, but *He is* The Light.

So, the next time you are given the chance to take center-stage, and all lights in the house are on you, remember whose shadow you're really standing in.

Do you enjoy having the spotlight? How does it make you feel to have the attention of a room full of people? Have you ever let the light of your own pride get in the way of how things really are? What did you do about it?

Into Everything I Hate

"I do not understand what I do. For what I want to do,
I do not do, but what I hate, I do." Romans 7:15

I know a good Christian guy who has a very strong addiction to chewing tobacco. He knows it is a disgusting habit and wants to quit, but the addiction has control. He absolutely hates being addicted to this disgusting vice.

I know people who have been addicted to cigarettes or alcohol, and many of them genuinely wanted to quit. They hate having ever gotten started on these gripping habits, but now they feel trapped by their own weaknesses.

I know how these people feel, and I sympathize. I am unavoidably addicted to sin. Our own sin is like a virtually unbeatable addiction. We hate what we do, and we hate ourselves when we do it, but too often we continue to act the same, nonetheless. No matter what our good intentions might be, we feel and seem powerless to resist that which we are called to hate.

But I have some good news. God is bigger and stronger than our addiction. I have a friend who once said, "Being addicted to something is like saying God isn't strong enough." I don't know how true that is, but it got me thinking. Can we really overcome addictions and sin? I think we can.

First, I have to realize whatever weakness I have is where I will be tempted. If smoking or drinking alcohol does not appeal to me, I probably won't be tempted in those areas, because that's where I'm strong. However, if I am tempted by lust or lying, I am much more likely to be attacked in those areas.

Next, realize God will always offer me a way out. Scripture tells me I will not be given more than I can handle.

So, prepare now, so you will be stronger when tempted by something you ultimately are called to hate as a believer in Christ. Good intentions are fine until it comes time to prove it. Will you do what you want to do, or will you do what you hate?

What do you have in your life that you hate but continually do anyway? What tempts you? How can you possibly overcome that temptation?

There She Goes

"But I tell you that anyone who looks at a woman lustfully has already committed adultery with her in his heart." Matthew 5:28

Today we're going to deal with a pretty tough topic. It's one that I face nearly every day—lust. Not only does today's society tell you that there is nothing wrong with lust, they even encourage it. If you don't believe me, turn on your regularly scheduled prime-time television sometime to see what I mean. You will see women dressed in clothes that are so revealing that I should be embarrassed to watch the program with my own mother. Why do they do this? It is because they know that if they dress women this way, they will attract more viewers. They know it will have this effect because the entertainment industry understands that we are people who lust.

I've told you about my trip to the beach. If you don't remember (or if you just skipped that page), I took my first real trip to the beach when I was seventeen years old, and—as expected—there were quite a few young ladies there who were more than happy to lend an eyeful to any watchful observer. This was a challenging situation for me, so I recruited a friend to hold me accountable for my "wandering eyes." I have a friend who has a subscription to *Sports Illustrated* magazine, and every year when that infamous swimsuit issue arrives, he immediately averts his eyes and throws it into the trash bin behind his building. He doesn't even want to deal with the temptation of lust. This is a mental problem that everyone deals with. In the book of Matthew, Jesus says that we don't have to have sex to commit adultery in our hearts. All we need to commit adultery are lustful eyes. I don't really know how it is for women, but guys have a *very* hard time with this very issue.

How do you deal with this? You can simply avert your eyes. That's a tough thing to do, but you will be proud of yourself if you do it. You could leave the room and take a breather if you need to. Usually, the best way to overcome temptations is to run away from them. If you are not where you can easily get out of, you could possibly do your best to think of something else that would in no way cause you to sin with your mind. This will not be an easy thing to overcome. I still struggle daily. But we must do this. Lust will eventually pollute our minds and create a barrier between us and our relationships with God.

Is it hard for you to keep your eyes and heart from lusting?

You Make Me Mad!

"A fool gives full vent to his anger, but a wise man keeps himself under control." Proverbs 29:11

I have a confession to make; I have a bit of a temper. It doesn't often show, and I am usually a pretty easy-going, mild-mannered type of dude. But every once in a while, things will start to build up inside me and then, it's only so long before something's got to give.

Recently, I found myself in a conversation with some people while simultaneously being pestered by my little brother. I stood there and did my best to ignore his juvenile attempts to engage me and listen to the people I was conversing with at the same time. It did not go as I had hoped. Ultimately, my anger won its battle, and I lost my temper, throwing myself into some stupid little battle with my younger brother in front of my friends and even my pastor! I must have looked like the imbecile of the month! I was so mad and embarrassed that I couldn't even think straight.

We all get mad sometimes. I have yet to meet someone that has never been mad about something. It's a very tough thing to control, but I must learn to overcome my temper.

What do you do when you get mad? My response to the situation with my brother was not the best way to go. I don't know exactly what would have been best, but what I did was definitely not it. I did, however, go back and apologize to my brother and my dad for losing my cool. I took a late night, mid-September swim in some really cold water, and I let myself cool off. At the time, it was exactly the therapy that I needed. Afterward, I felt just fine. I had gotten things fixed between God and me, my brother and me, and my dad and me. It bothered me no longer.

We are all easily provoked (some more easily than others), and we have to learn to control our tempers and emotions. I know I do. We can all get mad and heated up about something, but how many of us can be the wise man and keep it all under control?

Do you have a temper? How do you react when someone intentionally provokes you? Have you ever embarrassed yourself by losing your temper in front of a bunch of people? If so, didn't you wish you had been wise enough to control it?

The Little Red Devil

*"Likewise the tongue is a small part of the body,
but it makes great boasts. Consider what a great forest
is set on fire by a small spark." James 3:5*

I was sitting around one day, chatting with some friends. We were talking, and all of a sudden I found myself having said something that should have never been said. One of the girls—shocked and offended—got up and left the room, furious at my remarks. I felt awful. Then, one of the other girls turned to me and said, "You need to control that little red devil." I had never heard this expression, but she was referring to my tongue.

I have always had a problem with running my mouth when I should say something else—or probably nothing at all. In fact, I'm not completely sure, but I think I've probably offended just about every person that I know at one time or another. It's not that I enjoy making people upset. I just don't control my tongue well enough. In hindsight, I always realize what I probably should—or shouldn't—have said, but, obviously, by then it's too late.

Unfortunately, I am not the only person who has this disease of making a jerk of myself by putting my foot in my mouth. It's an international epidemic that almost everyone has to deal with sometime or another.

So, how can I know when to keep quiet? It's not always easy to do this, but maybe I could try to think *before* I speak. How many times could I have avoided hurting someone's feelings by just taking a moment to consider what was about to emerge from my mouth. There is a song by Chris Tomlin entitled "*Foot in My Mouth*," and it humorously describes a few situations where someone would have been much better off not saying anything at all. Now, this song was meant to be funny, but when it really happens, no one is laughing.

We all need to learn how to control what comes from our mouths. The sooner we tame the "little red devil," the more our relationships will grow and the better our lives will be.

When was the last time that you put your foot in your mouth? How did others respond? How did you feel afterward?

What–Me Worry?

*"Who of you by worrying can add a single hour
to his life?" Matthew 6:27*

I am such a worrier. Some days, it's as if the alarm sounds, my eyes gradually push their way to the "awake" position, and I am reminded of something that I seem to believe needs to be worried about. Did you catch that? I was typing pretty fast, so I wasn't sure. Even as I sit down to write this devotional, I have many concerns on my mind. Will it be good enough? Will it be applicable? Who will want to read this? Do you understand? I am plagued by my human need to control things, which causes me to worry about things that are out of my hands.

Even when I do have some control, I seem to overwork my mind with unneeded worry. "How many tickets do I need to buy for the next event?" "How can I improve my grades?" "Where will I go to college?" "What will I get out of my next summer?" I have come to the realization that this cycle never ends. It seems like everything has to be planned ahead, or else something will inevitably fall apart. Unfortunately, I am not the only person facing this useless application of stress. There are people all over the world who are inflicted with this awful need to worry. You may even be one of those people.

One reason people can't stop worrying is they refuse to put things in the hands of God. We feel we have to get things done on our own, or else they might not work out right. It all comes back to being patient and waiting for the perfect timing of our Heavenly Father. I can worry and fret about tomorrow, but—more likely than not—this will not solve my problem or extend my life. It only puts more stress on me.

God is in control, and when we all can get a good grip on that, our lives—*my* life—will be a lot less stressful and worrisome. Once we can stop worrying senselessly and start trusting God, we will have more enjoyable lives as believers in Christ.

Are you a big worrier? Do you put too much pressure on yourself? When was the last time that you put your concerns at the feet of God and allowed him to help you solve your dilemma? Try it, you might be surprised!

Who Are You Talking to?

*"Therefore confess your sins to each other
and pray for each other so that you may be healed.
The prayer of a righteous man
is powerful and effective." James 5:16*

You know, I've been to a bunch of Christian events in my young life, and I don't know if I've heard anything as much as I've heard evangelical speakers tell young people to witness to their friends. I've heard the question, "Why aren't you witnessing to your friends?" That is truly an excellent question. So, why do *you* think people don't share Christ with their friends?

I didn't know the absolute reason for this myself until recently. I know that some of the reasons are that we are afraid of being rejected or laughed at, or being considered an outcast by our peers, but would you like to know what it really boils down to? I was at a training seminar, and the instructor gave us this quote, "The reason people don't talk to their friends about God, is that they don't talk to God about their friends." Did you catch that? If not, read it again. Did you ever think that we are not sharing Christ with our friends because we aren't praying for them already?

When I was a senior in high school, we started a student-led outreach project in which we would each pray for one specific person for a month, and then, invite them to a meeting targeted toward nonbelievers. This gave us as students an open door and an opportunity to minister to the people in our school.

I can think of several times when I wanted to share my faith with someone, but I was afraid, unsure, and intimidated by what the other person may or may not say. Obviously, most of the time, sharing my faith is not an easy thing to do. So, I started praying for the people I was concerned about, and while not all of them have accepted Christ yet, I feel much more confident in presenting the Gospel to them.

It sounds so simple, doesn't it? Actually, it seems like this solution should have been staring me in the face all along, but I was just a little too blind to spot it. Maybe you've come to this conclusion already, or maybe this is a new idea for you. Either way, please keep praying for the lost people in your life. If you don't, it's likely that no one else will.

Can you think of anyone in your life that needs to accept Jesus Christ as their Savior? If so, start praying for them now.

Still Listening

*"I call on you, O God, for you will answer me;
give ear to me and hear my prayer." Psalm 17:6*

How well do you remember your childhood? Do you remember bedtime? When I was a young child, whenever he could, my dad would always say bedtime prayers with my brother and me before we went to bed at night. You know, even at such a young age, before I ever became a Christian, when I prayed I knew that God was listening. Did you ever have an experience like that? Do you remember how easy it was to believe that God was listening to you when you prayed at night? I do.

As we grow older, it is much more difficult for people to put their belief and trust in an unseen God. That childlike faith has faded like all of our other innocent perceptions. What many people don't realize and what gives me more comfort now than it did then is that He is still listening.

As our heavenly Father and our friend, God is eager to provide us with what we need and to lovingly listen to our calls to heaven. His love for us is so great that when we come to Him in fervent prayer, He smiles like a proud parent. I really can't understand how the mighty Creator of the whole world and the universe that surrounds it can hear someone as unworthy as myself. But, whether I am humbly asking for forgiveness for a wrong that I have done or I am desperately crying for His help, I know that He hears me.

He hears you, too. When any of God's children come to Him and humble themselves before Him, He listens with open ears. I take great comfort in the fact that the God I used to pray to as a young child still hears and loves me today.

How is your prayer life? Do you ever feel like you pray and God does not hear you, or maybe He just doesn't care? If so, how does that make you feel? When you pray, do you expect to see results?

In All Honesty

*"Therefore each of you must put off falsehood
and speak truthfully to his neighbor,
for we are all members of one body."* Ephesians 4:25

Sometimes, in the course of life, I feel like it would be better to tell a lie than confront someone with the actual truth. Why? Because people can get so defensive when you try to be honest with them. I'm not necessarily talking about lying today, but rather about being false in how you think and feel. We feel as long as we keep the peace with everyone in our lives, life will be grand. Well, it may be pleasant to tolerate, but it will never be truly authentic.

God wants us to tell the truth in all situations. Yes, there are various ways we can attempt to be honest, but few that will not draw conflict. How can we help to avoid conflict when being honest with people? Tell the truth in love. If you have a problem with someone, it may be better to approach that person by saying, "Look, I really value your friendship, and I don't mean to be critical, but I really was a little hurt when you _____," (You can fill in the blank.) rather than, "*What's wrong with you? Don't you have any consideration all? You must be pretty stupid to have done something like this!*" Now, this is a pretty extreme example, but do you understand what I'm trying to say? If you need to confront someone, it is always better to do it out of kindness.

Also, only dish it out if you can take it. What I mean by that is: if you are ready to be honest with people and confront them, be ready to be confronted. I don't like constructive criticism. I always ask for it, but usually I am eager to disregard it and get pretty defensive. This is something I am learning to deal with, because when I can lovingly accept what people have to say, then I can expect them to accept what I have to say. Though, sometimes they may be wrong. You don't have to submit or even agree with what others have to say, but at least you should try to listen and really hear what they're telling you.

What it all comes down to is this: we need to be honest with everyone, particularly with people we are close to. When we can be open and honest with those who are closest to us, we will have more tightly knit friendships.

Do you ever feel like you need to tell a friend something but don't want to because of what they may say? How do you accept criticism?

A Day Off

"Then he said to them, 'The Sabbath was made for man, not man for the Sabbath.'" Mark 2:27

Everyone needs to take a rest. We were not meant to work all of the time, and by no means does anybody want to work all the time. Everyone needs a day where they can take it easy. You might call this day the Sabbath.

I know what you're probably thinking. "Sunday is the Sabbath day." It may be, but that is not necessarily how it has to be. Think about this. If you are a pastor, a Sunday school teacher, or in almost any other ministerial profession, could Sunday be your Sabbath day? I've watched my pastor on Sunday morning, and believe me, he is not resting.

I was once in a Christian band, and we would many times be asked to come to a church or youth rally and play for a Sunday night crowd. When I was helping carry heavy amplifiers, speakers and other sound equipment, I was definitely not relaxing. For many people, Sunday just won't work as a suitable Sabbath day. It's okay for you to have another day to be your day of rest. The Sabbath is for you, not you for the Sabbath.

Now, please don't think that on your selected day of rest you can't do things like drive a car or make a sandwich, just try not to work so hard. Like the verse at the top of the previous page is saying, this was designed so you could rest and benefit from it, not so you could appear holy and super-spiritual to anyone who watches. You don't even have to stay at home. What I do when I want to relax is drive to Oklahoma City by myself (that takes about an hour) and spend the day there doing whatever I feel like doing. I'll go see a movie, go to a bookstore, grab a cup of coffee, or anything else that comes to mind. This is something I do because it helps me unwind and get away from my burdens and responsibilities for a while.

While sometimes emergencies may come up and make you unable to enjoy your appointed day of rest, I want to urge you to try your best to schedule days to recharge in whatever way works for you. Believe me, you will be glad you did.

Do you have trouble finding time to relax? Why is that? Have you tried to take a day and do whatever you feel like doing in order to recharge?

Life Is Precious

*"'Therefore I tell you, do not worry about your life,
what you will eat or drink; or about your body,
what you will wear. Is not life more important than
food, and the body more important than clothes?'"*
Matthew 6:25

About a month before my eighteenth birthday, I went through my very first bout with depression. Things were not working out the way I wanted. I was sick of school; I was falling out of communication with a good friend; I was frustrated with my music and, on top of everything else, I was having problems concerning girls. It was not one of the finest points of my life. Basically, I stopped appreciating life. I could not see all of the good God had done for me in my life; I could only see the hurt I was feeling at that stage of my life.

Recently, I was attending the final homecoming pep-assembly at my small school in Hinton, Oklahoma. Small town football homecoming in Hinton is a sight to see. Football players act as cheerleaders and do a cheer and a dance. A couple of good friends of mine were on the senior male cheerleading squad, and as I stood in the crowd watching my friends make hysterical spectacles of themselves, I began to smile. Not because I was in the midst of finishing my final year of high school, but because I was experiencing a moment of pure joy in which I watched some of my closest friends enjoy life. It was meant to be funny, but I found it very moving. I now realize I should be appreciating all of the time I have with these people, because soon, we will each go our separate ways.

Sometimes it's hard to realize how wonderful and precious this life really is. But it really is something to savor and take advantage of, as best we can. Jesus died so you and I could have an abundant life. That is, by the way, the greatest gift of all—life.

I have been learning that a big part of living is enjoying and loving life. I think of the ways God has blessed my life, and it makes me smile. So, I know whether things are up or down, this life is precious.

Do you sometimes feel like life is unfair and cruel? How do you deal with those feelings? Try to find things to thank God for, things you have maybe overlooked. You may realize how precious your life is.

I Get Down

*"May the God of hope fill you with all joy and peace as
you trust in him, so that you may overflow with hope
by the power of the Holy Spirit." Romans 15:13*

I n nineteen plus years of living, I have experienced my
fair share of bad days and rough times. Yes, I've flunked
a test that made the difference in a letter grade. And yes,
I've had a fight with a parent. Of course, someone of the
opposite sex has rejected me. Perhaps right now for you it's
something that it is a little tougher and harder to deal with,
like the death of a loved one or a divorce of someone you're
close to. These are things that can make you hurt and feel
down about yourself and your life.

You may have at one time or another dealt with depression—I have . . . once. I remember it as one the lowest points
in my life, emotionally. I felt like I had been abandoned by
everything I once held onto. Everything I felt was worth
something was fading away.

No one is above or beyond feeling bad about life. It
happens to everyone. I don't know a soul who hasn't cried
tears of sorrow and asked the question, "Why?"

But there is a happy ending to this sad and depressed
intro. Our God cares enough about us to help us go through
pain with hope. When I get down, the Lord is there to lift

me up again (sounds like a song, doesn't it?). He will give you strength when you are too weak to bear the burden. He will comfort you through tears of pain and sorrow. When you feel all alone in this life, God is willing to come and carry you through those hard times that you can't get through on your own.

I know sometimes it is hard to realize we have a comforter and friend in the bad times. When I am down and feel like I'm all alone, it doesn't seem like God could actually care about me. But He really is there, and He really does care about us when we need Him. He really wants to help.

Do you remember a time when you were weak and needed someone to comfort you through your tears? Can you remember being down and needing someone to pull you back on your feet? What did you do? Did you allow God to help you through that time of pain?

Thanks to the Friends

"Do not forsake your friends and the friends of your father, and do not go to your brother's house when disaster strikes you—better a neighbor nearby than a brother far away." Proverbs 27:10

The one thing people have in common universally is something you and everyone can probably appreciate— we all need friends. I know sometimes our "friends" are not really looking out for our best interests, and that is truly a tragedy. But a good friend is more valuable than gold. A good friend can be someone to listen to and talk to. They can be someone to laugh with and to cry with. A friend is someone we experience and appreciate life with. They are not to be taken for granted.

I do not have enough paper—nor do I have enough strength in my fingers—to describe how different friends have influenced my life and to express my gratitude to them for it. They have helped me through tough times and made my life much more interesting. I am truly grateful and blessed with the friends God has given me.

I am continually and truly amazed at how God has spoken to me in my life through different friends. It's because of a good friend that I continue to play the guitar. It's because of a good friend that I pursue my goals, when I feel like throwing in the towel. It's because of good friends that

I am writing this page right now. God has used so many people to reveal his purpose to me, and I am grateful for them.

This is ultimately a page of praise. First of all, it is meant to praise Jesus for being the ultimate friend and for putting great people in my life. Second, it is meant to give credit to those people who are good friends and to help both you and me appreciate the ones who make a difference. A good friend is a gift from God.

As I said earlier, Jesus is the ultimate friend and companion. He is always there for you and me, and he will never ever leave us. But He also provides us with irreplaceable people who give us earthly companionship—our friends.

Who is your best friend? What makes this person so special? How has God spoken to you through this person? Are you thankful for friendships you have been given?

You Know Better

*"For it is not the one who commends himself
who is approved, but the one whom
the Lord commends." 2 Corinthians 10:18*

We are all observers of other people, aren't we? We can't help but watch people living around us and passing us by every day, can we? We see how they live their lives, how they treat their friends and families, and how they act in their church environment. We watch, and we compare ourselves with everyone else in the world. We think we are doing okay because we are not doing something as bad as a neighbor or a friend is doing.

Just as I am watching other people, I know they are watching me as well. I am fully aware when I go to church, school, or anywhere else, that I am being sized up.

This happens because, as you know, if a person is doing something wrong, someone is eventually going to point it out. And when that happens, many times, people get very defensive. I know I do. I feel like a person is judging me, not trying to help me. Sometimes they are, but sometimes they aren't. When this happens, many people (myself included) start saying things like, "Well, at least I don't _____. You know, like so-and-so does." It all goes back to everyone trying to ease their guilt by telling themselves they aren't as bad as the guy or gal across the street.

So, instead of using other people to measure ourselves, we should read God's word and listen to His Spirit to see how we should be measuring ourselves.

The truth is simply that your neighbor is not the standard God has set for you or for anybody else. No one's life is graded on a curve, and we are not judged by how well or badly other people perform in their individual walks of life. He requires *your* best and not someone else's. So, instead of being as good as the guy or gal next to you, try to be the best God equipped you to be.

When have you shrugged off a conviction in your heart because someone else does the same thing you have been doing? How do you size yourself up against other believers?

My Confession

*"If we confess our sins, he is faithful and just
and will forgive us our sins
and purify us from all unrighteousness."* 1 John 1:9

Nobody likes to admit they are wrong. When I say something offensive and hurt someone's feelings, I hate to go to the person and say, "I shouldn't have said that. I was wrong. I'm sorry." I don't think anyone really likes doing it. But confession is a vital necessity to a healthy relationship with anyone—especially with God.

A lot of us have a strong tendency toward "blanket confessions." A blanket confession is when you pray to God and say, "Lord, please forgive me of all my sins. Amen." That was pretty painless, right? It takes no effort whatsoever. What about apologizing to other people? Which apology is better, "Hey, I'm really sorry you got your cheesy little feelings hurt, and I'm sorry you can't take a joke," or, "Listen, I didn't mean to hurt you. I was wrong. I'm sorry." It doesn't take a person of great wisdom to know which is the better apology, does it? God wants the same thing other people want—an honest confession and apology.

Think about it, God already knows when we've done something wrong, so it's not like we're going to hide it. Our confession is not for God's benefit. He doesn't need us to repent for what we have done, but *we* do need Him to forgive us, and we need to feel that forgiveness. Confession is so we can accept the grace of God's forgiveness for what we have done.

So, when we confess something to God—not as a blanket confession, but a real heart-wrenching gut-check—we become forgiven. He is not out to hold grudges or stay mad at you or me. He is ready to hear your confessions lovingly and forgive you. So, when I pray and I have something to confess, and I do it with a fervent heart, I know that I have been forgiven.

How honest do you think you've been with God? Do you need to confess something for which you need forgiveness? What could that be?

Have a Drink

"But whoever drinks the water I give him will never thirst. Indeed, the water I give him will become in him a spring of water welling up to eternal life." John 4:14

When I was seventeen, I spent the summer in Fort Worth, Texas. I truly experienced the good life that summer. I held a part-time job at Blockbuster Video, which provided the funding to allow me to do some really fun things. My friend, Greg, and I house-sat for two weeks. I spent time in the downtown areas with close friends. I went to a Texas Rangers' baseball game. I took two trips to Panama City Beach, Florida, and was given my first opportunity to lead music at a youth camp. It was, without a doubt, the best summer of my life so far. But something tragic happened in August—I had to go home, back to Oklahoma, where my experiences would only be memories of a good summer gone by too quickly. While it was a great summer, the bliss did not last forever. It inevitably came to an end.

I have a friend who loves Taco Bueno. When we go out to eat at Taco Bueno, I imagine it gives her a small taste of pure joy to bite into her favorite item from the menu. But, of course, eventually she will be hungry again.

Can you see where I'm headed? It is the same for us and our temporary bliss as it was for the woman at the well. It's not like she had never tasted water before, because she had, but that did not mean she would never be thirsty again. Jesus offered her and us living water, which is salvation. This is the gift of eternal life. This is something we will never run out of, nor will it ever expire. We are given something through Jesus we could never otherwise acquire, and that we will always have.

So, whatever joys you have going for you right now, they are no comparison to the joy and fulfillment you can receive from following Jesus and his commandments.

What makes you happy in life? What are some things that have made you happy and are now only a memory? How has salvation been different?

Drop Some Names

*"But if you show favoritism, you sin and are convicted
by the law as lawbreakers." James 2:9*

Okay, I'm as guilty of this one as anyone else. I often show heavy favoritism towards some people, and I have on occasion dropped names of people I wanted to be associated with. But don't, for a second, think I'm alone in this.

We all play favorites. I am usually not very willing to pull over to the side of the road and help out a stranger. I'm usually in such a hurry, or I'm just not up to helping someone change a tire. But I'll tell you this right now, if I was driving on the highway and saw Steven Curtis Chapman pulled off on the shoulder of the road, with his hazard blinkers on and a tire iron in his hand, I guarantee you I would be pulling over as quickly as I could to help out a man in need.

Now, please do not think I am saying you should risk your life by pulling over to help someone who could possibly harm you. Nor should you usually pick up hitchhikers. I'm saying I would be much quicker to help someone I was close to, or admired greatly, than someone whom I had never seen before in my life, or someone I didn't like.

How easy is it for me to help someone I like? Not too hard, huh? Anyone can show kindness to someone they like. But I am usually not as eager to assist someone I don't know or don't care for all that much. I once heard someone say the opposite of love is not hate, but indifference. Not caring at all about someone is actually worse than hating him or her. At least with hate there are strong emotions.

We are called as Christians to love everyone and to show it. I'm not talking about Barry White, turn-down-the-lights-and-listen-to-slow-music love. I'm talking about a Christ-like love, one of tenderness and compassion for other people.

Jesus never played favorites when it came to loving people, nor did He drop names to impress someone with who He knew or where He had been. He just loved others. He showed tenderness and compassion to those who would listen and accept. We should do the same.

When was the last time someone showed you a random act of kindness? Do you feel you sometimes show favoritism? How? Have you ever shown an act of kindness to a stranger?

Call Me Christian

*"By this all men will know that you are my disciples,
if you love one another." John 13:35*

As I have mentioned, I grew up in the very small town of Hinton, Oklahoma. And, as you may know, in many small towns, everyone knows who everyone else is and who their parents are. My dad was a pretty well known guy in Hinton, so, of course, I was the *son* of a pretty well known guy. I wasn't known as Rob, rather I was known as "the Carmack boy" or "the banker's son." In a way, I was known by association with my father. Throughout my years of growing up, I continually did things to make my father proud—and well, not so proud. This is how it is in one way or another for all of us.

When I was a youth-intern at Bear Valley Community Church in Colleyville, Texas, I took a group of young teenagers to camp, where everyone knew us by which church we came with. The actions of each group would either give their leaders a sense of pride or one of shame. The group I took made me as proud as a youth leader could be. We were all associated with the same church, and we wanted everyone to know how good the youth from Bear Valley really were.

As Christians, we bear the same responsibilities to Jesus. When we wear the name of Christ, we become associated with Christians everywhere. Because of this, we are commanded to show love to everyone. When we stumble, it's not just one or two people who take the hit, but everyone who has ever claimed the name of Christ.

It is a tremendous privilege to be called a Christian. Yes, here in the Bible belt it seems almost everyone who has ever stepped through the church doors claims they have some belief in God, but what good does that do you if you have not received his grace through salvation?

That is what makes us different, and according to Jesus, that is how people will know we are his children. It's through our love for others. I consider it an honor to be able to stand in front of large groups of people and say, "Call me Christian." It is the name I wear, and I want to make my Father in heaven as proud of me as I can.

Who do you associate with in your life? How do people see you? Who do you think you are making proud?

Cry Me a River

*"That night all the people of the community
raised their voices and wept aloud." Numbers 14:1*

I think we have all had our share of bad experiences and sad stories. No one is protected from tragedy and hard times. But how do we handle these hard times? Have you ever been at a funeral and heard someone say to the widow, children, or parents of the deceased, "Aren't you happy that Jim-Bob is home with Jesus? You shouldn't cry. If you cry, you are letting the enemy win the battle."

Then they quote Philippians 4:4, which says: "Rejoice in the Lord always. I will say it again: Rejoice!" I believe that this verse is used in the wrong context in such a situation. Yes, we are instructed to rejoice and be thankful servants, but that doesn't mean we are supposed to hide away our pain, for fear of being seen as unfaithful. When people are not allowed to cry and feel pain, it paves a road to denial. Also, denial takes away our ability to cry out to God.

We have been taught God has a plan, and we should never ask questions, just go with the program. On the contrary, questions help us grow in faith. Take a look at Psalms 73 and 74 in your Bible. These are the cries of a Psalmist with a broken heart; one who is not willing to simply hide his pain. It's okay to say in prayer, "God, I know that you're sovereign and graceful, but I don't think I deserve this. What's going on?"

God is listening with love, and He wants to embrace you and help you get through your tough times. It's time to stop denying our pain and stop pretending nothing hurts us.

It would probably also help you to talk to someone else about it. I can't tell you how good it feels to get things off of your chest and share your hurt and pain with another person. I have only gone through depression once in my life, and I hope to never experience that again. One thing that helped me to find my way out of that depression was to talk to someone.

A friend of mine named Jessie offered a sympathetic ear and comforting words to ease the pain I was facing. I can't tell you how much she helped me when I needed her friendship most.

Someday, you are going to hurt. So will I. When this happens, we can't hold back anything from the One who can help us through the pain.

What has caused you heartache? Were you able to be honest and allow God to heal you? How did you acknowledge your pain?

Table for Two

*"God sets the lonely in families,
he leads forth the prisoners with singing;
but the rebellious live in a sun-scorched land." Psalm 68:6*

I f you ask so many people what their greatest fear is, I guarantee one thing that will score very highly will be the idea of being alone. People are terrified they will end up with no one to love them and no one to give them the romance they want and feel they need. For most people, being alone is not a very appealing scenario. When everyone you know is in a relationship or getting married, who wants to be the one sitting alone at a table for two?

I have had this feeling. I know what it's like to feel so lonely your insides dully ache with some of the deepest emotional pains a person can feel. No one can help. It's the desire for a warm touch, close companionship, and the affection from another person which people long for.

I know a lot of people take things very lightly around this topic, because they see it as shallow and juvenile to have these feelings—especially in junior high and high school. I do not intend to make this mistake. It is in your teenage years that you become more vulnerable to emotions and deep feelings. Your heart can break at thirteen as easily as it can at thirty. If you will allow me to, I would like to tell you how you can better cope with this pain called loneliness.

Now, I am not by any means advising you to kiss dating goodbye or anything, okay? I am not going to push toward either dating or courtship, because that is not what this is about. However, I do want to tell you what I have learned. I have learned to use my singleness and to treasure it.

Somewhere along the road of life, we were tricked into believing if we don't have romance, then we need to find it. It starts being a necessity. I have friends who try to set me up with girls, because they think I need a girlfriend. I don't. I need only the things that will keep me alive and enhance my relationship with God. This is not to say we shouldn't date, but it is most certainly not a necessity, such as sleep and water.

I know it's often very hard to do, but try to trust that God will take care of you. Don't ever think He doesn't care about what you are going through. He does. But until He gets things working between Himself and you, you are not ready for Him to give you something great with a member of the opposite sex.

Have you ever felt lonely? How did you deal with it? Did you trust God?

A Word of Encouragement

"And let us consider how we may spur one another toward love and good deeds." Hebrews 10:24

A s I look back on my life so far, I curiously wonder where or who I would be without the encouragement of other people. It's an amazing thing, when you actually stop to think about it.

When I was a senior in high school, I was given my very first opportunity to preach in front of a church congregation—my home church, actually. Naturally, this being the church I was born and raised in, I was—to say the least—highly intimidated. I had spoken to a small youth group in Texas once or twice, but never to an entire church and especially not *my* entire church in Hinton, Oklahoma. But my pastor, Steve Murray, who had given me the opportunity from the very beginning, was willing to see me through it, to the very end. He coached me. He encouraged me. He met with me once a week right up to the day I was scheduled to preach. This was a much needed—and much appreciated—gift of encouragement, that I am, even now as I write on this page, most grateful for. You see, through Steve, I was—as the Bible puts it—"spurred" toward love and good deeds.

We all have this power. We can make someone feel good, confident, and worthwhile, simply by using our words. You can make someone's day just by giving him or her an encouraging word. Sometimes, we don't even realize we are doing it.

Sometimes, however, we feel we have to pull others down to make ourselves feel better. I recently watched a movie in which characters in the film performed cannibalism to gain strength. It was based upon an Indian tale where one warrior ate the flesh of another and gained the victim's strength. So, in order to become stronger, a man had to literally destroy another man.

And sometimes, that is what we do with our words too. We destroy another person to make ourselves feel better. Where did this fiction come from? I have come to realize it feels so much better to see someone succeed than to see him or her fail.

You have the power to encourage or to destroy. We should think about that before we open our mouths.

Who has encouraged you in your life? How did you feel? When have you been an encouragement to another person? How did it feel?

Can't Take the Pain

"For all have sinned and fall short of the glory of God, and are justified freely by his grace, through the redemption that came by Christ Jesus." Romans 3:23–24

One early morning, at about 3:30 A.M., a friend of mine came to my house in tears. She was overwhelmed with guilt by something she had done. She had given in to peer pressure and broken a promise made to both God and to her boyfriend. She was practically sick with guilt over what she had done and was sure her boyfriend would never forgive her. Through her tears, she continued to call herself a liar. She had already been forgiven once, how could she ask for it again?

We will all be tested with things that weaken us. Most of the time, these trials will come unannounced and intent on destroying us. It will never be easy for us to simply walk away from the sins we are accustomed to walking toward.

Let's take a look at Simon Peter. Jesus told him that he would deny he ever knew Him, three times. Peter, of course, swore he would never deny Jesus, no matter what (Luke 22:33–34). Well, that very night, Peter was asked three times if he knew Jesus, and his answer was the same every time— I don't know Him. The third time Peter denied, the rooster crowed, and Peter remembered what Jesus had told him only a few hours earlier. When this came to Peter's attention, he went outside and wept bitterly (Luke 22:54–62).

After Jesus had risen from the dead, He forgave Peter. They had just finished eating, and Jesus asked Peter if he loved him—three times. Each time Peter answered, "Yes, Lord, You know that I love You." Jesus gave Peter yet another chance to serve Him (John 21:15–19).

It's hard for us to take that kind of pain. I know that many times, when I do something I have promised God I would not do, I am consumed with guilt. I have, in effect, denied Jesus the same way Peter did. The most amazing part of this whole thing is that we have already been forgiven.

While Peter was denying Him, Jesus was taking the pain, guilt, and embarrassment of our sins with Him to the cross. He did this because He loves us, and He is willing to forgive us. We will all mess up a time or two, but we, as children of God, are already forgiven.

Have you felt guilty because of something you've done? What did you do? Have you asked for forgiveness? If not, why not?

Not Home Yet

"In my Father's house are many rooms;
if it were not so, I would have told you.
I am going there to prepare a place for you." John 14:2

One summer, I took a mission trip to York, Pennsylvania with a youth group from Georgia. I traveled a very long way to be a part of that, and it was more than worth it. We spent ten days eating, sleeping, praying, and living in the fellowship hall of a church in York. We became accustomed to that way of life. Most of us claimed that if we could have another day, week, or even month of this lifestyle, we would gladly accept it. We had grown so accustomed to this way of living after only ten days that we were not ready to give it up. This was not a home to any of us, but it very often felt like it. But I cannot tell you how wonderful a mattress felt to me after nearly two weeks of sleeping on a hard floor.

Have you ever gone somewhere to visit and not wanted to leave? I have. I have visited many people and places and, at the end of the trip, I was not eager to leave, even though I knew full well the place was not my home, and home has always welcomed me upon my return.

This earth is like the places we visit. We like it. We are very comfortable and accustomed to the lifestyles we have acquired, but it is not our eternal home. I know when I die, I will go home to be with my Father in heaven, and that is very exciting.

Now, don't get me wrong, I am not some sort of suicidal, crazy nut. I don't wake up every day hoping I will die. I enjoy my life. I try to appreciate it every chance I get. But I do not fear death, because I have been freed from that fear. The very minute I became a Christian, I was given a promise that I would not have anything to fear from death, because after this life, there is heaven.

But I won't lie to you—I am a little nervous. This is because I don't know what to expect. In my mind's eye, I can see Jesus smiling at me with His arms open wide. I can hear my Father saying, "Welcome home!" as I enter into His kingdom. Now, I don't want to sound too super-spiritual or anything of the sort. This is just how I picture my first glimpse of heaven.

I do like my life here on earth, but I should probably not get too content here. When I think about death, it comforts me to know I am not home yet.

Do you fear death? What makes you afraid? Does it comfort you to know that, if you are a Christian, you have a home waiting for you?

String Around My Finger

"Remember the wonders he has done, his miracles,
and the judgments he pronounced," Psalm 105:5

There are a few friends listed in my address book with whom I sometimes forget to keep in contact, when I should be writing or calling. I get so wrapped up in what I am doing, it just slips my mind. Then, without warning, I hear from them. One friend even sent me an email that said, "Rob? Are you dead? It's been a while." This reminded me to email him.

I have a friend named Jim. He is as forgetful as any person can be at such a young age. He remembers the most important things, but he tends to forget about the little things. One night he left his trigonometry book in the back of his El Camino during a rainstorm. The book was ruined. Now, Jim was not trying to destroy a textbook, he just forgot to get it. Sometimes, people need to remind him about things, so he won't forget.

Did your parents ever tell you if you wanted to remember something, you should tie a string around your finger, so you wouldn't forget? Sometimes, if I need to remember something, I write a note to myself on my hand. There is something in life we all need to remember that sometimes requires more than a string around a finger or a note on a palm. That something is the grace and love we are given with each breath we take.

Often, we each have trouble remembering these things. Sometimes, our hearts and spirits are broken, so God can get our attention and draw us back to Him.

One night, a friend came to me in tears. Her heart was completely broken, and she cried uncontrollably. We talked for hours, and throughout that conversation I continued to feel my emotions beginning to cave in. God used this friend to open my once calloused heart. I spent the remainder of the day examining myself. This friend may never fully know what she did for me, by choosing my shoulder to cry on. She was a very effective string that God tied tightly around the finger of my wounded soul.

We are so forgetful. How often do we overlook the grace and love we are given every day? One thing I have learned is, no matter how forgetful I am, God will use anything to be that string around my finger.

Have you been forgetful of God's goodness? Have you been taking things for granted? How has God reminded you in the past?

Garland of Grace

*"Blessed is the man who finds wisdom, the man
who gains understanding, for she is more profitable
than silver and yields better returns than gold."*
Proverbs 3:13–14

In each of our lives there is something we fervently strive after and pursue. For you, it might be a guy or a girl who has grabbed your attention, or it's good grades, fame, acceptance, or anything that could be a positive benefit to you in life. To one extent or another, I too have sought after all of the things listed above, at one time or another. But if there is one thing I have learned from seeking after these things that I think will make my life perfect for a time, it is that wisdom is the thing most worthy of pursuit. In your life, God is willing to help you, and how He intends to do that is to give you wisdom to use daily.

We see people all around who are in bad shape. Some are in the process of a divorce, some are in over their heads in debt, some have lost jobs and friends, and many of them will say, "God has dealt me an unfair hand! I don't deserve this!"

Now, wait just a second. While sometimes, a divorce is only the fault of one person in the marriage, more often than not, it takes two to tango—if you know what I mean. If someone is in debt, how do you figure they got there to begin with? God didn't overcharge on their credit cards for them, did he? God didn't stop anyone from making loan payments. If someone has been fired from a job, was it God who prevented him or her from being a model employee? Was it God who made him lose his temper and jeopardize a friendship? I think you get my point. We often shoot ourselves in the foot by simply being too foolish to deal with things in life. Why is it we are so foolish? It is because we lack wisdom.

The book of Proverbs is full of down-to-earth wisdom for everyday life. Read the verse at the top of the previous page again. It says wisdom is more profitable than silver and yields better returns than gold. In short, wisdom is a priceless asset to be acquired. If you will pursue and embrace the wisdom God provides through His word and through other people, it will benefit your life. You can count on it.

When have you found yourself in need of wisdom? Can you think of any time you reacted with foolishness instead of wisdom? If so, how could you have changed it? When can you use wisdom in life?

The Discovery of Church

*"Let us not give up meeting together, as some
are in the habit of doing, but let us
encourage one another—and all the more
as you see the Day approaching." Hebrews 10:25*

L et me pick your brain for a second. What is your idea of church? When I say the word, "church," what do you think of? Were you raised in the traditional church setting, or is the whole thing pretty new to you? I can imagine you more than likely think about dressing up really nice, sitting in pews, singing old hymns, passing the offering plate, stained glass windows, and maybe, nodding off during some message about how if you're not a Christian you're going to burn. Did I come very close to what you thought of? This is something we may call church, but let me assure you, it was intended to be much more.

While our world may have stereotyped church in the ways described above, we don't really need stained glass, pews, hymns, nice clothes, or any of the other cosmetic things we visualize when discussing church. The only thing we need to have is the presence of God and each other.

When I was eighteen years old, I worked for a church in a Ft. Worth, Texas, suburb. This church did not have any of the elements described above. In fact, they held their weekly Sunday morning services in the auditorium of an elementary school. People wore clothes that they would have worn to a movie or a football game—they came just as they were. They came to experience God as a family of believers.

I participate in a small group that meets every other week or so. There are six of us. When we gather together, we do so to earnestly seek to grow and learn about God and to encourage each other to do the same. We spend time growing together and sharing together—this is also church. A church is not made by bricks and mortar, but by Christians who come together as real people, to praise and serve God. You may think that you have experienced church, but if you have lived your life as a pew-packer who goes on Sunday morning, only because someone forces you, or because you feel obligated, you have missed out on one of the greatest blessings God gives us, and that is the gift of the church.

Have you ever experienced real church? If so, when? If not, what do you think is missing?

That Kind of Love

*"This is love: not that we loved God,
but that he loved us and sent his Son
as an atoning sacrifice for our sins." 1 John 4:10*

D o you comprehend the love a parent has for their child? I don't. The reason I don't is very simple; I am not a parent, nor have I ever claimed to have some deep understanding of what it feels like to be a father or a mother. In the same way, I do not understand the kind of love God has for us, His children, because (obviously) I am not God.

I don't know why Jesus would give up His home in paradise to spend thirty-three years here on earth, to be treated like scum and eventually put to death in the most painful and humiliating way possible. He was beaten within an inch of His life, and He was hung naked on a cross to die. He did this because He loved us. He did this because He loves *me*. This is true love. The more I think about it, this page is more a devotional on confusion than anything else, because I don't understand that kind of love.

Our love, as people, is weak, and it pales in comparison to the love God has for us. We are flimsy and self-serving. We let marriages fall apart; we drift away from other people; we see friendships ruined every day, because we just don't know what kind of love lasts. Usually our love, in short, is conditional.

But God's love is without condition. Whenever we begin to fall or waver, He doesn't say, "That's it! I've had it! I can't love a person like this." Rather, He seeks to carry us when we are incapable of walking on our own, and His love wants to renew our hearts. His love for us is patient, kind, honest, and eternal. He takes the good with the bad and hopes we will allow Him to make us better.

This is very confusing for me to try to grasp. You may have it all figured out, but I am at a constant loss of comprehension when it comes to this topic. No, I don't know how that kind of love exists, but, fortunately, I know where it comes from.

Have you ever thought about the kind of love only God can offer to someone? How does it compare to the love that we, as people, show to each other? How can we improve?

Studying for the Test

"I have hidden your word in my heart
that I might not sin against you." Psalm 119:11

My junior year of high school was by far the most try-ing year for me. I had the most challenging class schedule I'd had in all my years of school to date. One of my more difficult classes (not that they all weren't difficult) was Biology II. The teacher was Mr. Meriwether, and he was an advocate of challenging students to use their brains in the classroom.

Being a beginner with this whole "use your brain" con-cept, I initially didn't do very well in his class. It was one of the hardest I have ever taken. I depended on learning only when I was in the classroom and thinking this alone would help me pass the tests. Unfortunately, I was wrong. He put things on tests that we had never discussed in class! He gave us a short review and expected *us* to go home and learn.

I didn't catch on as quickly as some of the other stu-dents, but one day I was prompted to take my materials home and actually try to study. I did this, and miraculously I passed the next test. Not only did I pass, I even made an *A*. I never realized how significant studying really was. It made it much easier to pass the test. Now, you may be saying, "Duh, Rob.

Everyone knows the best way to pass a test is to study." Then why don't more people do it?

This is much like the Word of God. We face tests in our lives every day, but we continue to neglect to do the studying required for us to be able to pass. The Bible is full of wisdom and life-lessons for us to gather and learn from. There are true stories for us to use as tools to learn how to deal with life, such as the story of David and Bathsheba, the story of Joseph's perseverance in doing the right thing, the story of Esther's courage in a difficult time, and so many more.

There are words of wisdom compiled in the book of Proverbs. We are given guidelines for life throughout the entire New Testament, by Paul, and by Jesus Christ himself.

I am convinced, if I really want to pass the tests this world has for me, I am going to have to study. You have this choice to make as well. If we will listen to God's Word, He will lead us in the right direction.

How often do you read your Bible? Do you ever find it easier to find answers and wisdom when you have been faithfully studying?

A Special Gift

*"Each one should use whatever gift he has received
to serve others, faithfully administering God's grace
in its various forms."* 1 Peter 4:10

When I was eighteen, I took a Spiritual Gifts Assessment Test. After answering over one hundred thirty questions, the test revealed I have the gifts of Administration, Creative Communication, and Leadership. As I examine experiences of my life, I see where I have been given many opportunities to use each of these gifts.

For example, I got to oversee the summer youth ministry of a growing church in the Dallas/Ft. Worth metroplex, giving me the chance to do administration. Many opportunities to lead worship in song on my guitar and also to speak to churches and youth groups let me use creative communication. Also, when the youth ministry I worked on went to camp, I got to lead twelve students and four volunteer workers.

We all have special gifts given to us by God. We each have different desires and talents, making us special to our Creator. No two people are exactly the same in this area. No one has the identical set of passions and gifts as another person. Earlier I mentioned the gifts that I *do* have; well allow me to let you in on something: I am not gifted at all in the areas of Craftsmanship or Mercy. These are two things I have no interest in, nor do I have any desire to pursue them. Some people are incredibly gifted in these areas. Some can take a few pieces of wood, a box of nails, and a hammer to make a beautiful chair. Some listen to people's heartaches and complaints and honestly cry with them, showing a merciful spirit. No one is the same. We are all, however, part of the same body of believers.

On your physical body, don't the eyes, hands, mouth, and ears help each other do their own job more effectively? In the same way, we can complement each other's weaknesses with our strengths.

No Christian is without spiritual gifts. We are all gifted in some way. Find out what you are passionate about and what you like. This will probably have something to do with your gift. God is ready to use you.

What do you think your spiritual gifts are? What are you passionate about? What kind of work would you be best at?

A Slug's Life

"How long will you lie there, you sluggard?
When will you get up from your sleep?" Proverbs 6:9

There is something out there that very many people will openly admit to being guilty of—procrastination. I am not an exception. I am as guilty—if not more so—as the next person. In fact, writing these devotionals has tried my tendency as an active procrastinator. There are some days I don't feel like writing anything, or maybe I just don't feel like I have anything to say. However, I have found if I think and pray long and hard enough, something will most often come to me. But whether it is homework, chores, or any other duties involving a deadline, many of us seem to live by the motto "I'll do it later."

Now, some people don't have this problem at all. Some folks get so busy and wrapped up in everything they can find time for, they simply don't have time to procrastinate. In fact, some of them probably wish they had the luxury of procrastination.

A good friend of mine is like this. He is class president, Student Council president, FCA treasurer, and he plays football and basketball. He sings in honor choirs all year round. He's some kind of officer for FFA, but honestly I couldn't tell what his title is. He is one busy dude. But this type of behavior can be just as dangerous as the lazy, procrastinating type. I'm not saying this friend of mine is committing a grave sin by being involved in a lot of activities, but it does create difficulties.

Either way, a relationship with God can be jeopardized. If you sway toward the lazy side, you should know we are called to work and to be laborers, to get things done when they need to be done, and to be faithful in our relationship with the Lord. It is never healthy to put things off until the last minute.

Or, if you are one of those "go-getter" types, you may find you don't have time for a relationship with God. You may be ultra-busy all the time, but it seems you may slack off in a most important area of your life. Both types of behavior are being what the Bible calls a "sluggard."

So, don't hesitate. Take the initiative and recognize what is most important. Refuse to be a slug any more.

Do you find you procrastinate or are too busy? Does this affect your relationship with God? If so, what can you do to help it?

More Than Gold

*"Similarly, if anyone competes as an athlete,
he does not receive the victor's crown
unless he competes according to the rules." 2 Timothy 2:5*

Very few people would consider themselves strangers to the realm of a competitive nature. In my little hometown of Hinton, the high school football team is so revered the whole town gets involved—especially if they are winning. The competition runs wild in the fall, during football season, in this otherwise sleepy, little town.

I know a youth pastor who is a phenomenal volleyball player. Every summer he takes his youth group to a camp where there is an annual tradition of a sponsor's volleyball tournament. In his early years of student ministry, his whole week at camp revolved around the tournament. And every other sponsor from every other church knew if they had to play against this guy, he would make their time on the court miserable. He was out for blood! I have heard this man tell his story a time or two. He says that even though he realized how he was alienating the other sponsors, and though he has recently cleaned up his act, it is still a tough thing for him to get out there and have the Christ-like attitude, which he always told his youth to have. This guy became so consumed with winning, he forgot why he was at camp to begin with.

Now, there is nothing wrong with a little healthy competition, if the game is played in a positive way, allowing the players to represent Christ. If you are competing, play with your whole heart and try to win. Just don't let yourself get out of hand.

I am sure you have seen either the Summer or Winter Olympics, haven't you? It is a great thing for an athlete to participate. We all want to see our flag flown high for the world to see. Every athlete who participates wants more than anything to win a gold medal.

So, if and when you compete, do it bearing the image of Christ, like an Olympic athlete carries the colors and flag of their native country. When you do this, win or lose, you will receive more than gold.

Do you have a competitive nature? Have you ever noticed yourself taking the competition a little too seriously? Have you ever embarrassed yourself and your teammates? What do you think the best attitude on a playing field should be?

Nice Folks Finish First

"A kind man benefits himself, but a cruel man brings trouble on himself." Proverbs 11:17

I have a natural tendency to offend people. In fact, I would say there are very few people who know me very well whom I have not offended at least once since I have known them. I don't know why I do it, but I end up doing and saying things which make people feel bad. But I'll tell you something—I usually feel much worse than the people I offend. I can't tell you how much I dislike myself when I have done such a thing to another person.

Recently, I've been trying something new. Instead of making rude comments to people, I keep my mouth shut. Instead of being mean to people, I'm nice. And you know what? People have noticed. I've noticed also, when I do good things for someone else, I feel good too. I can't fully describe how nice it feels to make other people feel good about themselves.

So, now I've started showing random acts of kindness to strangers. When I see someone walking into a building I am also going into, I hold the door open for him or her. I have become a more gracious driver, letting other drivers into the lane in front of me. It simply feels good to do good things for people.

Do you remember the story of the Good Samaritan? If not, check out the parable in Luke 10. It tells of a man who was traveling and came across a guy who had been robbed and beaten within an inch of his life. The Samaritan delayed his trip and took the beaten man to an inn. He paid the innkeeper to take care of the stranger. He had never seen this guy in his life, but he still stopped everything to help out a fellow man in need. He did not have to stop. Two other travelers had already passed this guy and left him there to die. But this Samaritan didn't do that. He saved the man's life with a random act of kindness and selflessness. Do you think the Samaritan felt burdened by this battered victim? I seriously doubt it.

Nothing can compare to the joy received from helping a needy person. I will admit that helping another person out of a situation will not solve the world's problems, but it will make the world seem much nicer to you and to the person you helped.

Do you see yourself as a kind person? How do you feel when you make someone else feel good? Is it more satisfying than being cruel?

Wrestling Angels

"For where you have envy and selfish ambition,
there you find disorder and every evil practice."
James 3:16

We sure are ambitious folks, aren't we? We are so concerned with our success. We want more than anything to "arrive" and make our ambitious, self-absorbed mark on the world as we know it. This is a dog-eat-dog world, and we are all capable of becoming puppy chow to those who want a prize more than we do. We have convinced ourselves we have to be the first and the best at everything. We want to do things our way. We want God to work around our schedule. His plan will have to wait until we have climbed every mountain that seems to stand in our way.

But let me tell you about a guy named Jacob (If you want, you can look up his story in Genesis, chapters 25–33). Jacob was one ambitious guy. From reading his story, it seems like he was always trying to play ahead of the game. Even when Jacob was born, he was found grasping the heel of his twin brother, vying to be the first out of the womb. When they were older, he shrewdly traded food for his brother Esau's birthright when Esau was starving. Later on in his life, he and his mother conspired to trick his father

Isaac. He told blind Isaac that he was Esau, and Isaac gave Jacob the blessing he had intended to give Esau. Even when he was beginning to grow old, Jacob found himself literally in a wrestling match with God himself. They tussled all night long, and after all this time of wresting, Jacob demanded a blessing.

Yes, you could say that Jacob was a pretty ambitious guy. He knew God had a plan for him, but he did not want to wait for God to provide the means. Perhaps this is why Jacob found himself working for fourteen years to obtain the woman he loved. God must have been teaching Jacob a lesson in patience, which he so obviously needed.

Sometimes we find ourselves wrestling with God too. We want to control our lives and everything in them. We don't seem to be able to trust God enough to provide us with what we need, so we decide (foolishly) that we won't wait for God; we'll just do it ourselves.

If I can make a suggestion based on a few of my own experiences, give in and stop wrestling. God has a better plan, just be patient.

Do you find you are continually trying to get ahead of everyone else? If so, have you tried to be patient and stop wrestling?

Developing Self-Discipline

*"Whoever loves discipline loves knowledge,
but he who hates correction is stupid."* Proverbs 12:1

As far back as I can remember, I have wanted to do well in a field of music. So, when I was about fourteen years old, my dad bought me a guitar from a clearance sale at a music store. I went to the band director at the high school and asked him if he would teach me to play. I discovered something a little discouraging in my first lesson— I had absolutely no natural musical talent whatsoever. I had no rhythm, no coordination, and absolutely no natural ear for playing a song. Quite frankly, I stunk! I became so frustrated I could hardly stand to think about it. But I still wanted to learn to play. So, I continued to take lessons.

It took over a year, but I actually started to improve, and the better I got, the more I would practice. I continued to grow in my skill, and today, I still play and try to improve myself a little every day. But none of this could have been done without self-discipline.

Self-discipline is something we all need. Very rarely will you see anyone succeed at anything without a little bit of self-discipline. If we want to acquire this, we must first identify our goals and aim high to achieve them. Ask yourself,

"What do I want?" Whether it is athletic skill, good grades, musical ability, or anything else, it will usually require a good bit of discipline.

This is also true in your relationship with God. I'll be honest, I don't always feel like having my quiet time, but because I have disciplined myself to spend time with God every day, it is not even an option as to whether or not I will do it.

Decide ahead of time that you will accomplish a goal. Decide to work out more, study harder, practice longer, or anything else needed to accomplish your goal. But decide now, no matter what, you will spend time with God. If you can acquire self-discipline in that, you will be blessed.

Do you feel like you are self-disciplined? Where do you need work?

The Heart of Worship

"Then those who were in the boat worshiped him,
saying, 'Truly you are the Son of God.'" Matthew 14:33

After many opportunities to stand in front of a group—large or small—and lead Christians in singing praise and worship music, I find I really enjoy doing it. But sometimes (actually most of the time), I get too wrapped up and involved in the musical portion. I wonder things like, "Am I singing in tune?" or "Am I playing this guitar part right?" or "Do these people like me?" I end up getting so involved in those types of thoughts that I tend to let the real reason for doing it slip by me.

But the truth is, God does not require us to always sing on pitch or to play the guitar with such skill as to win a Grammy. A song in itself is not what is required of us. Worship is a much deeper journey into our own hearts. The song is just a method. If I am too concerned about the music to be worshipping, it just becomes another tune.

We also have a tendency to forget why we worship in the first place. It is not for other people to see what holy and good Christians we are. People usually tend to equate the word "worship" with singing catchy and uplifting songs. The songs are great, but the singing itself is not worship.

So, you are probably wondering what I think worship is. The act of worshiping is acknowledging who God is and what He has done for you. When you do anything with the pure intent of serving God and acknowledging Him by your actions, you are participating in worship.

So, when I am leading music and I get distracted by how I think the people in the audience are seeing me, I am losing something very precious, and that is the authentic worship of singing songs together as believers.

It is not easy to put things aside and participate in a true worship experience, but it can be done. It is an experience that will fill you through and through. In genuine worship, God will bless your heart.

Do you feel like you have ever participated in true worship? How do you acknowledge God when you gather with other Christians? Do things distract you? How do you feel you can worship God?

You Then Me

*"Sitting down, Jesus called the Twelve and said,
'If anyone wants to be first, he must be the very last,
and the servant of all.'" Mark 9:35*

When we were young children, my younger brother John and I had quite a few little squabbles, as brothers will do. One thing we must have fought over more than anything was who would get to sit in the front seat of the car when we were going somewhere. It never mattered if we were driving two blocks or twenty miles; we would consistently battle over that front seat.

Think about it. When you're a kid, you are always looked at as just a child. But it seemed as though the front seat held some sort of special power that would make you seem much older and more important than you would have visualized yourself from the back seat. This contest for power begins in the hearts of children. The sad thing is there are many people who live their entire lives this way. They spend every day of their lives trying to beat someone to that metaphorical front seat. They act as if life is one big contest.

That is a true shame. We are such a selfish breed of people; some feel they cannot be successful unless someone else is an utter failure. We are willing to walk all over others to get one more step ahead of someone else. This, I'm afraid, is not the way to successfully live your life.

When Jesus washed the feet of the disciples, He didn't say to them, "Okay, here's how it works. You all wash *My* feet, and then I'll wash yours." That is not how it worked at all. Jesus voluntarily, without any prompting, got down and washed the feet of His friends. He expected no reward for this gesture of kindness; He simply did it out of unselfishness.

If we could all be a little kinder to people and willing to step out of the way and let someone else ride "shotgun," things would be so much different than they are now. If we could say to someone, "You can be first, I'll be last," we would not only bless them by our kindness, but we would receive a blessing too, because there is an internal satisfaction in having given unselfishly. Humility and selflessness are Christ-like methods of showing goodness to His people.

Have you found yourself fighting for a specific "front seat" in your life? How has it affected you? What can you do to be selfless toward other people?

Long Way to Run

*"Therefore let us leave the elementary teachings
about Christ and go on to maturity,
not laying again the foundation of repentance from acts
that lead to death, and of faith in God," Hebrews 6:1*

As I write this page, I am within six months of graduating from high school. I have spent the majority of my life learning and growing, to prepare for this event. But even though I will be out of high school and smarter than I have ever been in my life, I am not even close to being finished with all my education. I still have college to look forward to.

You know, even after I finish college, I still won't have learned all that I can possibly know. Some people go on to graduate school, to get their master degrees. And even after that, some go on to get a Ph.D. in some field that I'm sure they feel they have conquered mentally.

But not so fast. There are a lot of folks who have already earned those Ph.D. diplomas and have also received a little bit of that thing most valuable to any student—life experience. It seems like you can never reach an intellectual finish line at which you have finally learned everything there is to learn. That is because we never stop learning. I heard one person say, "Once you've stopped learning, you are probably dead."

We have been called to grow in maturity and faith in Jesus. Much like in the race for knowledge, no one can reach their quota in maturity and faith. We can never possess so much that it is enough. No matter where we are spiritually, we still have a long way to go before we can count ourselves righteous enough for God. In fact, it is impossible. No matter how much we grow, we can always grow a little more.

So, how do you grow? In having your daily quiet time with God, you are growing in your faith and maturity. Also, when you spend time with other believers who are spiritually more mature than you are, you will no doubt find yourself learning things from them. We are to press on to build our relationship with God.

So, we must understand, there is no finish line here on earth. We will never find ourselves doing a victory dance this side of heaven. But the rewards received from seeking to know God more daily will be worth the run.

How have you been growing lately? Do you feel like you have been improving your relationship with God? Why or why not?

Hands and Feet

*"For we are God's workmanship, created in Christ Jesus
to do good works, which God prepared in advance
for us to do." Ephesians 2:10*

Take a quick look at yourself for a second or two—inside and out. What do you see? Physically and mentally, how many different tools do you have to work with, right there at your disposal? No one is without something to work with, whether it is a strong pair of hands to do physical service or an encouraging tongue from which people receive positive support.

The point is, you were made to do something besides sit in your comfortable recliner, watching television all day long. We were created for service. No one was created with the design to do absolutely nothing with his or her life. People are not designed for a shelf. We are all given opportunities to act as God's hands and feet, in service of Him. These opportunities should not be looked upon as drudgery, because they are a blessing we should be thankful for. The fact that God wants to use *me* to do something for Him is so humbling, when looked at from the appropriate perspective.

But we must realize also, God does not *need* you nor does He *need* me to do His work for Him. His plans are not ruined if I refuse to comply with His will. In fact, if you or

I flat-out refuse to do the work God has given us the opportunity to do, He'll do it some other way. The loss is ours, because we are the ones who are missing the blessing of being a servant to the God of the universe.

Look at all the men who helped write the Bible. They were eagerly doing God's will, allowing themselves to be His hands and feet. Because they were obedient, they were given the opportunity to help write the most widely read and distributed book of all time. They all probably said, "You are great; I am weak. Make me strong enough to serve You. Let me be Your hands and feet."

We are each given opportunities and abilities to serve God effectively. Not one person is born without that. But we must become willing servants. If you are a Christian, God is going to want you to act as His hands and feet. Don't miss out on this opportunity.

Do you feel as though you are a faithful servant? Are you willing to be God's hands and feet to serve Him more effectively? If not, what is stopping you?

Nothing at All

> *"Do not let any unwholesome talk come out*
> *of your mouths, but only what is helpful*
> *for building others up according to their needs,*
> *that it may benefit those who listen."* Ephesians 4:29

I grew up in a small town, where everyone knows everyone else. There are a lot of really good elements to a small town, and Hinton, Oklahoma, is one of the greatest communities in America. But one big, bad thing that most (if not all) small towns possess is the overwhelming ability to gossip. It seems when everyone knows everyone, everyone *talks* about everyone, and sometimes what they say isn't so good.

You will always hear things like, "He's a drunk," "She's a snob," "Did you know that they are cheating on each other?" This goes on and on and seemingly never stops. Sometimes, it can really bring you down, to realize how cold-hearted people can be behind other people's backs.

Do you remember the movie *Bambi*? Try to remember the little rabbit named Thumper. He would always refer back to the wise words given to him by his elder: "Mama says, 'If you can't say anything good, don't say nuthin' at all!'" Now, his grammar may be a little less than perfect, but the message is made of solid gold. Maybe your mama gave you the same advice. "If you can't say anything good, don't say anything at all!" This is a true-to-life lesson everyone needs to take a hard look at.

One reason I am so adamant about this particular lesson is simply that I have experienced a bit of this myself. More than once, I have heard through the grapevine that someone slandered me and distorted my image as a person and as a Christian, throughout the school and, sometimes, the whole town. Honestly, it really hurts to discover this.

I am very active in my church youth group and FCA, so when people look at me the way these rumors would have them believe, it not only hurts me, but it hurts every ministry I represent. When this is done to anyone, it is worthless and harmful filth.

Now, I know I cannot go around the entire town or school trying to stop all gossip, like I'm Batman, trying to save Gotham City. I cannot tame anyone else's tongue. All I can do is simply keep my own mouth shut. In fact, it is what I am commanded to do. So, if I can't say anything good, I won't say nuthin' at all!

Do you feel that you are a gossip? Whom have you hurt with your words?

It Is Well

"Cast all your anxiety on him because he cares for you."
1 Peter 5:7

I have seen many people face immense tragedy, in my lifetime. I have seen families go through painful divorces, as hate enters where love was once present. I have seen children lose parents to suicide. I have seen a loving son watch his father go through heart surgery, praying that the father would come out alive. I have seen a mother carry a baby for nine months only to find her child was not alive at the time of delivery. These are horrible tragedies, which might make some people ask, "Does God really exist? How could He watch me go through these horrible things and not do anything? I thought He was supposed to care about me!" I think we all know life is no stranger to tragedy.

I cannot explain why bad things happen to good people. I wish I knew, because then I could easily justify my faith. But the fact is, I cannot explain the pains and hardships people go through.

But I do know one thing for certain; God does love us, despite what cynical and hurt people think. And while He doesn't always shield us from pain, He can always carry us through that pain.

People are so shaken when confronted with a death or any other tragedy life finds a way to throw in their direction. Things like this never come with much—if any—warning. There you are, minding your own business, when—BAM! Something comes from out of nowhere and knocks you face-down. We stop believing bad things only happen to other people, and finally understand we are potential victims to pain just as the person next to us.

Some people's biggest fear is death. They are terrified that some day they will wake up for very the last time. I am glad I don't have to worry about this. I'm not saying I won't ever die—at least on earth. I simply know that when I do die, I am going to be taken care of for eternity. I am not very enthusiastic to find out exactly *how* I will meet my end, but the final result is a happy ending.

I look ahead, and I see hope. I look forward to seeing all that I'd merely believed in by blind faith, when my eyes will really be open. I will see what I once could only believe in. It is this kind of thinking that lets me say, "It is well with my soul."

How do you deal with tragedy? Does it test your faith? Are you afraid to die? Be honest. What could give you peace?

Underdog

*"The Lord said to Gideon, 'You have too many men
for me to deliver Midian into their hands.
In order that Israel may not boast against me
that her own strength has saved her,'" Judges 7:2*

Did you ever see any of the *Rocky* movies? I can really get into those. For one thing, I love to watch boxing. (I could never actually do it, but it's fun to watch.) For another thing, Rocky was always the underdog of the story. He was never the heavy favorite, and people can really root for that. It seems we almost always have a tendency to cheer for the guy who is the underdog of the battle.

God is also like this. Throughout the entire Old Testament, He continually used people no one would think were suited for the job. Take a look for yourself. You've got Gideon (from whose story we get the passage at the top of the page); Joseph (who spent years in prison before receiving a promotion to second in command to Pharaoh); Esther (a young Jewish peasant girl who became Queen of Persia); Moses (a sheep-herding runaway who was called to lead the nation of Israel out of Egyptian slavery); and David (the young shepherd boy who defeated the warrior giant, Goliath and became king of Israel).

Why do you think God is so partial to those who seem to be on the short end of the stick? What makes Him so particular toward underdogs? It's so people will know God is in control, not people. If every time God wanted something done He picked a "Superman" type of person to do it, how would we know who actually won the battle—God or Superman? But when He gives power to the powerless, He makes it obvious that God, not man, did the work.

Also, this is done so we can see that God can and will use anyone who is faithful and willing to listen to His voice and follow His instructions. With your spiritual gifts and a faithful heart, God will use you to do amazing things.

But, in serving God, humility is necessary so everyone will know who has really been winning the battles. I'll tell you this: There is something good about seeing the underdog come out on top, don't you think?

Do you ever feel like the underdog in your life? Have you been willing to allow God to use you? Do you ever feel like any of the biblical characters listed above? Why or why not?

Blind Lead the Blind

"He also told them this parable: 'Can a blind man lead a blind man? Will they not both fall into a pit?'" Luke 6:39

I will be honest—I am terrible at math. I struggle so hard in everything that has to do with math. It is embarrassing. Let me set a scene for you. Let's say I'm sitting in whatever high school math class I happen to be taking. I'm scratching my head, tapping my pencil in frustration, and I'm about to pull out my hair for total lack of understanding of anything that has any relationship to mathematics. Then, all of a sudden, someone comes into the classroom and tells me I have been appointed the new professor of Complex Analysis (a *really* tough math course) at Massachusetts Institute of Technology. (I'll continue when you're through laughing.) Obviously, I'm not exactly qualified to lead this course. In fact, I would probably be just as effective at teaching a classroom full of people how to speak Martian.

Yes, we can all get a good laugh at this. But the truth is, this type of thing is happening all over the place. There are people everywhere who are claiming to be enlightened and superior when it comes to things of a "religious" nature.

High school teachers are telling you we are all creatures of evolution. College professors are saying God could not "logically" exist. We read prominent authors who ridicule religion. Some politicians tell us the church is for the weak-minded. Hollywood presents Christians in film and television as either crazy fanatics or hypocrites. Blind leaders are guiding our blind society.

We must be careful not to be led by these deceptions. First of all, don't be afraid to ask questions. Some may ridicule you and accuse you of being ignorant, but remaining inquisitive is a key to not being led by the blind. This is a dangerous place. A place where lies are made to sound as though they are the gospel truth, but in reality they are still lies. No one is incapable of being deceived.

When the lost are leading, everyone will inevitably get lost as well. We have got to keep our eyes open, so we don't allow ourselves to fall into deception. Don't allow yourself to be led by the blind.

What kind of deceptions have you heard? Were you compelled to believe them? What did you conclude? Have you ever allowed someone else's leading to get you lost in confusion and frustration?

A True Friend

"A friend loves at all times,
and a brother is born for adversity." Proverbs 17:17

When people start to talk about friends, I have to crack a tiny smile, because I know I have been especially blessed in this area. In my hometown, there is a group of good Christian guys I spend the majority of my time with. I can proudly say they are my friends. In the metroplex of Ft. Worth, Texas, God has led me across the path of some truly amazing people, from whom I have learned a good deal of life's more important lessons. I am privileged to say these people are my friends as well.

Also, all the way over in Athens, Georgia, there is a group of people whom I have been given the great blessing of knowing. Every time I go somewhere, I come to appreciate the people with whom I develop friendships. Some are deeper than others, but I do consider each a friend. This is not because I have an electric personality, but because God has allowed me to know some truly great people here in His world.

As I am sure you know, the types of friendships you have will vary from person to person. Some are just acquaintances, people whose names you know and say "hello" to in the hall between classes. Some go a little deeper in that you spend extracurricular time with them. They go with you when a group goes to the movies or to a concert. After them comes the innermost circle, and we see people who truly affect our lives. These are the ones who are closest to us and in whom we confide.

All these are important. None are dispensable. But the group that affects us most is that which stands the closest to who we are—the group at the center of the circle. They are the hardest to come by and the most valued. These are friends who will keep your secrets and will not spread rumors. The more friendships we can develop like this, the healthier we will be.

I will be honest. There are not a lot of people who fit this description for me. I do not open up very easily and am not quick to trust anyone. But the people I do trust and confide in are those for whom I am especially grateful. They have taught me how to be a friend and how to love life.

So, in conclusion, make friendships that matter. These are the people who will see you through your toughest times.

Who are your closest friends? Do they encourage you in your Christian life?

Remember Your Chains

"But if anyone does not have them,
he is nearsighted and blind, and has forgotten
that he has been cleansed from his past sins." 2 Peter 1:9

Does it seem to you like people have short-term memories? They can only remember things that have happened most recently. Now, you may be saying, "I have a great memory. I can remember things from when I was just a little older than a baby." That may be true. We don't have a problem remembering *what* happens in our lives, but rather how we felt as a result of these occurrences. But it's hard to remember exactly what made you so starry-eyed over a certain guy or girl after you have been together for an extended amount of time.

I have read accounts of people who have been in prison. If there is one thing that runs parallel with them all, it is they didn't care for the whole prison atmosphere. Another thing they seem to agree on is they are determined to never go back to that horrible place from which they have been released.

As Christians, we have been released from a prison cell called sin and death. When I received Christ into my heart, a gate was flung open, and I was pronounced *free* from the power of death and sin for all eternity. That was the day I was forever released from prison. After a while, we seem to forget the full gravity of that cell, and what it could be like if we had never been freed. But I can promise you that most—probably all—ex-prisoners do not forget the pain and suffering of prison. Why are we so careless with a much more significant and lasting release?

I have begun to think to myself, "Where was I before God's grace took over my life?" It's a mighty pitiful sight. I was, first and foremost, the biggest hypocrite I had ever seen. I was confused as to what life was supposed to consist of, and everything I wanted was strictly for *me*. In the midst of a huge family, I was lonely. I felt I was worthless. I was so insecure I would be rude and cold to everyone, so I could feel just a little bit of power. I hate the person I was within the walls of my cell.

But then I was released. And what a beautiful day that was. But, if I have really been set free, why do I sometimes act as though I am still chained to the things that once bound me?

Where were you before Jesus set you free? Do you ever act like you are still a prisoner? Have you forgotten your chains?

What Good...?

*"What good is it for a man to gain the whole world,
and yet lose or forfeit his very self?"* Luke 9:25

In the past few years I have seen a large number of people graduate from either high school or college. And I have noticed when you ask someone who is stepping into a new realm, "What do you want most out of your life?" They will more likely than not tell you they want to be successful. Some say it as if it were the single most important thing they could do to make their existence worthwhile: "I want to have my dream home." "I want to drive the car of my dreams." "All I want is to have a swimming pool, and I'll be happy." These are the phrases of a people who are confused about what should be more important than any success ever acquired. But really, who *doesn't* want to be successful? Did you ever hear someone say they want to be a miserable failure?

I'm sorry to tell you, but there are many people who have been highly successful and still are not happy with their lives. I hear people say things like, "I can't feel sorry for *that guy*. He makes more money in a day by playing professional baseball than I do in ten *years!*" But does that make a person an instant success in the whole scheme of life? I don't think so. There have been many highly successful celebrities who have dealt seriously with depression and suicide. They may seem to have everything while, in reality, their lives are falling apart. These people probably have sat up at night and wondered, "What is this all about? What am I doing with my life?"

Now, by no means is success a bad thing. But it should not be the most important part of our lives. We should learn this lesson now, before greed takes hold of us and corrupts who we are. When people get too busy in their lives, they do not have time to focus on doing the things that make life worth living. Serving God is an amazing part of life, and people miss this because they are too wrapped up in climbing that mountain of ambition.

Slow down. Take a look around at the life you have. You may not be dealing with things like ambition and greed now, but don't wait until you are. Decide now that whether or not you gain the whole world in success, you will not forfeit your very soul for it.

What do you want to do with your life? Is success the only thing important to you? What matters most in your life?

Hold on to Jesus

*"Not that I have already obtained all this,
or have already been made perfect, but I press on
to take hold of that for which Christ Jesus
took hold of me." Philippians 3:12*

You may find yourself going through life as your normal routine leads you, with no potholes or obstructions to get in your way. Many times, something huge may rock the whole boat and disrupt you and, very often, your relationship with God. Someone may die; you may find yourself in the hospital; your family may be falling apart. I don't know. But I do know that many times these kinds of jabs can sorely interfere with how things are, between you and God. You may even begin to question your faith.

Don't think I haven't asked questions about why I believe what I believe, because I have. I have lost friendships, relationships with females, loved ones, and opportunities in my limited amount of time here on this earth, and there have been many times when I questioned whether or not I am holding onto air.

It begins to be very hard to hang on to your faith at some times in life. And Satan uses them to draw us away from the Lord. He wants us to question our faith and loosen our grip on our beliefs. Our enemy does not want us to grow strong and learn in a healthy relationship with God. He wants us to fail, and he will use anything he can to make it happen.

There are quite a few people who refuse to strive for a spiritual mountaintop experience, without a fun event to surround it. I have noticed that in order for some to continue growing, they need constant activity. They act as though they cannot grow from their quiet time apart from other believers. To them, their Christian walk centers around church camps and retreats. They are activity-driven. They can only hold on when they are placed in an environment where Christian growth is constantly encouraged. I've often noticed that the time between Christmas and summer is hard for this type of person.

I want to encourage you, no matter what season of the year it is, and no matter how hard the enemy tries to pull you, hold on—even cling—to the hand of your Savior. Most of the time it will not be very easy, but please, don't loosen your grip.

What pulls you away from your relationship with God? How can you hold on?

Good Life

> *"What is more, I consider everything a loss
> compared to the surpassing greatness
> of knowing Christ Jesus my Lord, for whose sake
> I have lost all things. I consider them rubbish,
> that I may gain Christ." Philippians 3:8*

I once heard a Christian speaker say to a group of young people, "God wants to ruin your life." I couldn't help but think, *What is that supposed to mean? Why is he telling them this?* But he was right. No matter how good our life may seem to us, God can do better. Sometimes, this requires a lot of really big changes.

You may have some kind of plans for yourself in the future, and they may be exactly in tune with God's will. However, I do know one which didn't work out quite the way I initially wanted it to.

A few years ago, all I wanted to do was to be an actor. I had a naive dream of moving to Hollywood and becoming a big movie star. I would have done it, too (or died trying), but God had better plans. He dissected my whole life and point of view, but I can tell you that now I have no desire to ever be an actor. I decided to pursue a career in Christian ministry instead.

There was another time, after I had decided to go into the ministry, I was sure I was supposed to go to Baltimore,

Maryland, to help a friend start a church for non-believers. I was so sure of it; I was determined not to let even the will of God get in the way of these plans. Well, the friend who wanted to do this slowly became less of an influence on me, and now we seldom speak. This was not easy. I loved this guy. All I wanted to do was go to Maryland and live the good life in starting a new church, but this was not in accordance with God's will. So He solved the problem by eliminating the source.

This experience helped me to realize that pain can often be what brings you into the arms of happiness. I hated losing that friendship, but I have become much more in tune with what God tells me through my quiet time. Think about it. When you are lonely, you find yourself looking for someone to love, and God is there. When you lose a close friend and find yourself needing a true friend, God is there.

So, don't hold back your "decent" life, even if it seems just fine, because God may have something better. His plan is always the best.

What pain has brought you closer to God? Has your life improved as you have allowed your life to be changed? If so, how?

Godsend

"A student is not above his teacher, but everyone who is fully trained will be like his teacher." Luke 6:40

The summer before my junior year in high school was a pivotal time. Within that three-month period, God altered the entire course of my life. The most amazing thing is that He used mainly one person to generate this change. I was already a Christian, but the teachings and influence of a young seminary student named Greg changed the way I looked at life, religion, relationships, and everything else you can think of. It was during this time period that I decided to pursue a life in full-time Christian ministry. I also discovered a love for leading worship with my guitar, which had never even occurred to me before. All of this happened because of the influence of Greg. I have no doubt God placed Greg in my life for this time to do exactly what he did for me. I believe he was sent to mold me for use in the ministry. Greg was definitely a Godsend (a person in my path who had the ability to make an incredible difference to me).

I have seen married people who are so effective in serving the Lord as a couple. They allow their gifts and opportunities to complement each other, and God is free to work because of it. These people have been given a priceless gift in each other. God gave each to the other, so they could help mold and encourage each other. We all have been given Godsends. These people who walk with us are invaluable. They shape our personalities, and it is through them that we see what it is to be a follower of Christ. They teach us things through their words and influence us with their own lives.

Many people have greatly influenced me. In fact, there are too many to mention. Some are sent as a means of encouragement, when I feel like I can't go on any longer. Some are sent to teach lessons in loss. Some have been sent to teach me how to be a friend, and some were sent to teach humility. Whoever it may be, I am thankful for these people whom God has sent to shape and mold my life, as He would have it.

Who do you feel has been a Godsend in your life? Who influences you the most? Do you think you have had this effect on anyone else?

Walk on Water

"He replied, 'Because you have so little faith.
I tell you the truth, if you have faith as small
as a mustard seed, you can say to this mountain,
"Move from here to there" and it will move.
Nothing will be impossible for you.'" Matthew 17:20

I have a young cousin named Summer. Like most small children, Summer is quick to believe almost anything a grown-up tells her. I remember one time when her mother was having a garage sale, and Summer's uncle said her mother had sold her to a customer. Summer ran into the house with tears in her eyes, begging her mother not to sell her. Now, of course her mother didn't *really* sell her, and if someone had said something like that to you or me, it would seem ridiculous. But a child is dependent, not on what seems logical, but on what people lead her to believe. Summer didn't use reasoning to know her uncle was playing with her; she just naturally believed he was telling her the truth.

Do you remember how blindly you could believe anything an adult would say when you were younger? You didn't ask "how" or "why," because you would naturally assume they were older and knew what they were talking about. Why would they ever deceive you? Remember how easy it was for you to believe in Santa Claus and the Tooth Fairy?

As children, we didn't take time to ask if things made any sense. We just believed.

We should have that childlike faith when it comes to trusting God too. Peter did, sort of. When Jesus was walking on the water, Peter was the only one with enough faith to actually step out of the boat and trust that Jesus would not let him sink. It didn't last long, though. He took his eyes off of Jesus and began to sink. But there were eleven other guys in the boat who didn't even think about stepping out onto the sea. Peter had that childlike faith, which Jesus said could move mountains.

I'll be honest. It's not easy to simply believe. Sometimes, simply believing does not make any sense. The entire secular world will tell you you're wasting your time with all of this "God stuff." They think if they can't see it, it must not be there. What a false assumption! God has given us plenty of reasons to believe. The lives we live and the people around us are reasons. I'll tell you this, though. If you truly believe, you will be able to move the mountains in your life.

Do you have trouble with your faith? What stands in your way?

114 - Box of Letters

Just a Little Bit

*"Show proper respect to everyone: Love the brotherhood
of believers, fear God, honor the king." 1 Peter 2:17*

W hile growing up, one of my favorite things to do at the end of the week was to stay up late on Saturdays and watch *Saturday Night Live*. In my younger years, I used to roll around on the floor, laughing at the weekly comedy offered by this age-old television show. But as I think about the elements which made the show so funny, I see they constantly made fun of anyone and everyone who was a potential target of the media. The humor on that show—more often than not—was generated through making fun of others. While there are millions of people who think that this is hilarious (and I have had my share of laughs), we must realize this is not right. The fact is, we should respect everyone—even if they don't deserve it. As true followers of Christ, we are to show respect to all.

Let's take a look at our president, for example. There are a large number of people who think he is dishonorable, dishonest, and unworthy of any respect. But whether these allegations are true or not, he is still our president. He still holds the highest office in the country, and we are to respect him for what that office represents. But we tend to show respect only when we feel like it.

You may go to school and show a great deal of respect to your principal, or to your boss at work (at least to their faces). But when you go out to eat, do you show the proper respect to the waitress who brings your food? She may be slow or discourteous, but for all you know, she is working her second shift of the day because her replacement called in sick. And maybe her two kids are being watched by a crabby old neighbor who would rather be watching soap operas than watching her attention-starved children.

Everyone you come in contact with needs respect and the Bible specifically says to respect your parents. The Bible specifically says to respect all authority figures. That means teachers, principals, police officers, and employers. The Bible says to show respect to everyone. That means store clerks, gas station attendants, waitresses, and (Oh No!) even telemarketers. But why should I respect these people? It's simple—because *I* want people to respect me.

To whom do you not show respect? Do you think you deserve respect?

Man of God

"Blessed are they whose transgressions are forgiven, whose sins are covered. Blessed is the man whose sin the Lord will never count against him." Romans 4:7–8

When I was a youth-intern in Texas, the youth group I was working with went to camp. On the final day of camp, I experienced more stress than on any other day of my life. I won't bore you with all the details, but let's just say it was *really* stressful.

That night, while I was finally clearing away all the obstacles and could finally go to group time with my church, one more person wanted to have my attention for a minute. About five different people relayed the message that I was to go downstairs to see this man, and while I was standing in the elevator, waiting for the doors to close, my good friend Heather said, "Rob, you need to go downstairs." I'm embarrassed to say I snapped. "I'm in the elevator! Where do you think I am going!" I barked back at her. In hindsight, I was not happy with myself about what I had said or how I had said it, and—obviously—neither was Heather. I had to go back and apologize for my rudeness, and because she is a good friend, she forgave me.

Have you ever heard the phrase, "Nobody's perfect"? Well, in case you were wondering, that is true. There is no person on this earth who is without a flaw. I know many good Christian people—true servants of Christ—who have messed up at some point in their lives. They never claimed to be perfect. They are still human and still face trials in life.

As much as I wish I were a perfect Christian, I'm sorry to say I am not. I'm sorry to say that sometimes I lose my temper and make a complete fool of myself. There have been moments in my life when I have lied—whether they were huge whoppers or little white lies makes no difference. Sometimes I put my foot in my mouth and create barriers between someone I care about and myself. But there are times in my life when I am doing exactly what I need to be doing. Sometimes I'm a man of God, and sometimes I'm just another messed-up sheep.

I want to be in Christian ministry. This is the profession I have chosen to pursue. In it, I know people will see me as a "man of God", but it will not always be true. I will always do my best, but when I don't, I know God will always be willing to forgive me.

Where do you possess weakness? Where are you most likely to stumble?

Famous Last Words

*"But whoever disowns me before men, I will disown him
before my Father in heaven." Matthew 10:33*

One day I went on a journey to a college campus with a
friend named Jonathan. The reason we were going,
however, was not to attend class, but to witness to
lost people whom we had never met. We were sharing the
Gospel with total strangers. Talk about a day out of your
comfort zone. I can't tell you how frustrated and dismayed
I was to see that no one came to know Christ that day. I
knew *I* didn't know how to share my faith with strangers,
but I thought Jonathan was a pro! I thought surely he would
know some profound way of leading a new acquaintance
to Christ. I watched every person we talked to turn away
and reject the greatest gift that could ever be given. It could
have been their only opportunity to be led to Christ and
live forever in paradise! How could they walk away? I was
so discouraged.

But this happens every day. People all over the world
reject the Good News of Jesus for some of the most inane
reasons. Many of them say, "I'm just not ready, yet." Some
say they do not want to give up the life they are living, and
they know that being a Christian will make them change

who they are. They are afraid they will have to stop smoking weed and drinking beer. They don't want to give up their nightlife for the gift of eternal life. Some stand in church and fidget during the invitation and say to themselves, "I don't want to make everyone stand here for another verse of *Holy, Holy, Holy.* Maybe I'll go down *next* week." These weak excuses often turn out to be the famous last words of someone who was never ready or didn't want to change.

People think there will be plenty of time for this whole "Jesus thing" later. They think they will have their whole lives to become Christians. They forget that no one is guaranteed to see tomorrow. No one lives forever.

People you know are making these tragic decisions every day. You may sit next to them in school, or you might see them when you go to work. They are everywhere, and they are dying. When someone tells you they don't want to hear about Jesus, those could be their famous last words.

Do you know someone who is not a Christian? What do they say when you tell them about Jesus? Have you been praying for them?

Splinters and All

*"And anyone who does not carry his cross
and follow me cannot be my disciple."* Luke 14:27

I know a young lady who decided to be a journeyman (sort of like a missionary, but for less time). She was sent to Brazil, and decided on the first day she had made a big mistake because she absolutely *hated* being there. It was very hard for her to adapt to a new culture, and she felt completely out of place for about the first two weeks. But she was determined to stay with it and refused to quit. As time went on, she felt God was using her, and she began to enjoy where she was and what she was doing. If you asked her today, she would say without a doubt it was God's will that she go to Brazil.

Now, I'll be the first person to tell you the Christian life is full of great and wonderful benefits and blessings. I would not want to live my life any other way. But we must realize that this life does have its share of hardships and pain. Very rarely is it ever easy to be a growing disciple of Christ. We face criticism. We feel disappointed when we see someone turn away from the truth of the gospel. We feel intense heartache when we see a non-Christian pass away. We say painful good-byes when God calls us to live and work in a new environment.

I know a girl who dated a guy for over a year. One day, she felt convicted she had been devoting all her time to her boyfriend and none to a growing relationship with God. She loved her boyfriend, but she knew without a growing relationship with God, she would never be truly happy. So, with a heavy heart, she ended her long-time relationship. She was happier in the long run, but at the time her heart was broken. It was so hard to do what she knew was the right thing.

As Christians, we have to be willing to experience our share of hardships. This is not because God wants to mess us up, but because He wants to make us better than we are now. Knowing pain now will help us be happier in the long run. But we each have to carry that cross—splinters and all.

What hard times have you experienced? Have you ever had your heart broken? How does that experience affect you now? What is the toughest thing you have ever had to face?

Showing Some Responsibility

"For each one should carry his own load." Galatians 6:5

here are quite a few things in this world I have absolutely no control over whatsoever. Things such as the weather, the stock market, and who will win the next Super Bowl are completely out of my hands. One thing I cannot and never will be able to control (and neither will you) is other people, and what they do.

So, what can I control? Quite frankly, I think controlling myself is plenty for me to handle. I have control over how I respond to trials in my life. Everything I do is because I willed it to be so. Everywhere, people are claiming, "I am a victim!" They try to convince us they are not responsible for themselves. I have heard of burglars who got hurt while breaking into a house and then sued the homeowner. Hardened criminals blame society for their behavior and claim they were created by an unfair system of government. This lack of responsibility is disturbing.

So, how can I be responsible? That's a fair question. Let me ask you this, how do you spend your money? Are you wise with it, or are you impulsive when you buy? I'll be honest. By nature, I am a very impulsive buyer. I usually don't think about how wise it would be to save my money, and I come back to a product when I have plenty of cash to blow. We live in a fast-food culture where we are encouraged to spend frivolously, and I am guilty of this very thing.

I can also show responsibility by how I respond in certain situations. I have been advised to delay responses to situations in which I may get angry. We are told that counting to ten is a good idea. It may not always help, but at least it is a start. If I just start spouting words of meanness and anger, then I have burned bridges and built walls between the subject of my raving and me.

The final way is one you hear about from your parents. You know, the one about being punctual and doing things you are required to do (such as homework, household chores, taking care of your possessions, etc.). These are things people will see as taking responsibility.

Being responsible—while not always easy or fun—is a rewarding thing that will improve your life.

Do you think that you are a responsible person? When in your life have you been responsible? When have you not been responsible?

An Everyday Evangelist

*"In the same way, I tell you,
there is rejoicing in the presence of the angels of God
over one sinner who repents." Luke 15:10*

W hat is your mental picture of a stereotypical evangelist? Is it a man who wears nice, expensive suits, flashy jewelry, helmet-like hair, and a perfect smile as he shakes your hand and speaks in a deep, charming, (and probably fake) southern accent? Is it someone who stands at the front of churches, shouting and telling people that if they do not come forward *right now*, they are in danger of hell (probably pronounced *hale*)? Does this resemble your mental image of an evangelist? This certainly is not a stereotype without prime examples. I have seen some myself. Now, we are taught we should *all* be evangelists. Does this mean that we should make people annoyed and afraid of Christianity? I don't think so.

Do you ever feel guilty for not talking to total strangers about becoming a Christian? If so, I don't think you should be so hard on yourself. I used to do this all the time. I would get on an airplane and sit down next to someone I had never met in my life. Immediately, I would begin to ask myself if I should try to share the Gospel with them. Because I am not usually very bold with complete strangers, I would always delay talking to my seat-neighbor. Inevitably, I would leave the plane, having not said a word to the person next to me, and I would feel guilty. I have come to realize I should not be so demanding of myself. Some people have the undeniable gift of evangelizing strangers—I don't. I need to get to know the person first. I feel they have to be able to trust me before I can try to change their lives.

This is not the only way to be an evangelist. Sometimes, all you need to do is invite a lost friend to a church service. I have a friend who helps people as his exercise of evangelism. He will carry books and even push wheelchairs when necessary. These are also methods of evangelism.

So, don't let anyone make you feel guilty for not being Billy Graham, because guilt is a lousy motivator. Just try to identify the very best way for you to share Christ with someone. This may be boldly sharing the Gospel, but it also may be serving or inviting someone who is lost. Whatever works for you, do it, because we are all supposed to be evangelists.

In what area are you most effective as an evangelist? Have you ever felt guilty for not doing more? If so, why did you feel this way?

Somewhere Down the Road

"'For I know the plans I have for you,' declares the Lord,
'plans to prosper you and not to harm you,
plans to give you hope and a future.'" Jeremiah 29:11

As I look back at my journal from the past year or so, I find fervent prayers that were faithfully answered, in due time. They were answered after I had suffered intense frustration and dissatisfaction with some things in life. In hindsight, it is easy for me to see why God made me wait for an answer. I can see the learning I developed from the pain and uncertainty of situations that are now but memories of heartache, yet once seemed so real. I can see how God used these things to shape and mold me into a better person. Of course, I could not see it at these specific times, but I learned a great deal from almost every difficult situation I have been through.

Let me give you an illustration. A couple of years ago, I drove to Colorado with my family on a ski trip. It took over fourteen hours of driving. A good part of this "road-time" was endured on a long stretch of New Mexico highway that runs straight through the desert for an unbelievably long distance. I absolutely *hate* that part of the drive, but it is an unavoidable part of the journey that eventually leads to a beautiful mountaintop.

I see a lot of this in my journey of life. I want to make it to the mountain but hate the hard parts of the trip. We don't realize the narrow road of Christianity is sometimes hard to travel. We can hurt and cry, but we still have to endure the journey. It is hard for us to see that, even though it is difficult now, somewhere down the road the joy of staying on our path will be worth the pain once suffered from the difficulties of the trip.

God will provide answers to our questions of confusion. He has greater plans for us than we can grasp, as of yet. We may not understand it now, but we will. Somewhere down the road, everything will be clearer.

What parts of your Christian journey have been hard on you? Have you ever wondered how God was using your experiences to broaden your horizons? What pains have you experienced that may have taught you something useful in your life?

Unanswered Prayers

*"And he who searches our hearts knows
the mind of the Spirit, because the Spirit intercedes
for the saints, in accordance with God's will." Romans 8:27*

D o you keep a journal? I have been filing through old entries in mine, thinking about some of my most fervent prayers of weeks and months past, and I can find a few which were never really answered—or at least not answered with, "Yes." But something a bit puzzling is I am actually glad these petitions were never given the attention I once desired for them to receive. I see the goodness in God's decisions to say, "No" to some of my requests. I realize He knows when I have prayed for something that will not benefit me in His overall plan. He's not neglecting me but rather protecting me from my own supplications.

Before the end of my junior year of high school, I prayed for an internship at a large church, located almost halfway across the country. This was not a *bad* prayer, but it still was not the right thing for my life. That door of opportunity closed on me, and I did not receive the job. But it turned out that God needed me somewhere else, where I would be much more useful. Instead of going across the country to be someone's gopher, God placed me in a church in Ft. Worth, Texas, to work with students who had no youth pastor. It was one of the most blessed summers of my life, and I owe it all to an unanswered prayer. I owe it to God for loving me enough to say, "No."

God always answers faithful prayers of those who serve and love Him. But sometimes the answer is, "No." He does this because He loves us so much that He has to withhold certain things for which we may ask, but this does not mean we should not pray. A healthy relationship requires communication, and if you want to build a strong connection with God, you must talk to Him and allow Him to speak to you.

So, don't think He's not listening just because your wishes aren't granted. God is not a genie. He is like a good parent; and like a good parent, He knows what is best for us. So, be sure to thank God for unanswered prayers—even if you don't know why.

What prayers of yours have not been answered? Why do you think this is? Can you look back and see God's wisdom with respect to any of your prayers you thought went unanswered?

Topical Index

Accountability: 19, 55
Ambition: 141, 165
Anger: 83
Association: 111
Being an Example: 15, 29, 177
Being Gullible: 37, 159
Being Judgmental: 65
Bible Study: 131
Blame: 47, 71
Body of Believers: 19
Church: 127
Commitment: 35
Comparing Yourself: 103
Competitiveness: 137
Confession: 33, 105
Decisions: 25
Death: 121
Depression: 99
Emotions: 113
Encouragement: 117
End Times: 13
Faith: 57, 167, 173, 187
Friends: 101, 161, 171
Forgiveness: 33
God's Grace: 11, 67, 107, 163
God's Love: 9, 129
Guilt: 119
Hard Times: 47, 169
Honesty: 93
Humility: 7, 23, 147

Kindness: 139
Laziness: 135
Loneliness: 115
Lust: 81
Peace: 13, 69
Playing Favorites: 109
Prayer: 25, 51, 89, 91, 189
Pride: 37, 45, 77
Priorities: 41
Quiet Times: 5
Reminders: 123
Respect: 175
Responsibility: 183
Sabbath Day: 95
Salvation: 11
Self Esteem: 27
Self Sacrifice: 59, 143
Service: 49, 53, 57, 61, 73, 151, 157, 181
Sin: 79
Spiritual Gifts: 133
Spiritual Growth: 17, 69, 149
Thankfulness: 31, 43
Value of Life: 21, 31, 97
Wisdom: 39, 125
Witnessing: 15, 179, 185
Words: 85, 153
Worry: 21, 87
Worship: 7, 63, 75, 145

To order additional copies of

Box of Letters

Have your credit card ready and call

(877) 421-READ (7323)

or send $9.95 each + $4.95* S&H to

WinePress Publishing
PO Box 428
Enumclaw, WA 98022

online orders: www.winepresspub.com

*add $1.00 S&H for each additional book ordered